4/00

MOLDOVA

Patricia Sheehan

MARSHALL CAVENDISH
New York • London • Sydney

Reference edition published 2000 by
Marshall Cavendish Corporation
99 White Plains Road
Tarrytown
New York 10591

© Times Media Private Limited 2000

Originated and designed by
Times Books International, an imprint of
Times Media Private Limited, a member of the
Times Publishing Group

Printed in Malaysia

Library of Congress Cataloging-in-Publication Data:

Sheehan, Patricia, 1954-
    Moldova / Patricia Sheehan.
        p. cm. — (Cultures of the world)
    Includes bibliographical references and index.
    ISBN 0-7614-0997-1 (lib. bdg.)
    1. Moldova—Juvenile literature. I. Title. II. Series.

DK509.56 .S53 2000
947.6—dc21   99-053433
                          CIP
                           AC

INTRODUCTION

MOLDOVA IS A NEWLY INDEPENDENT STATE situated between Romania and Ukraine in southeastern Europe. Once a province of Romania, it came under Soviet rule in 1940 and remained one of the smallest Soviet republics until the collapse of communism in 1991. An independent Moldovan republic was established on August 27, 1991. The country has since embarked on a series of economic, social, and political reforms. It is slowly working toward its aim of becoming a democratic society.

The 1990s have been a challenging time for Moldovans. Ethnic conflicts are proving difficult to resolve permanently, and the political and economic issues relating to establishing a market economy look insurmountable. Nevertheless the people are resilient after centuries of struggle. Today they are proud of their country's independence and ability to assert their culture and national identity.

CONTENTS

A woman peddler selling fruits beside a highway.

3 INTRODUCTION

7 GEOGRAPHY
Physical environment • Rivers • Climate and seasons • Flora • Fauna • Environmental issues • Cities

19 HISTORY
Early history • Moldavia and the Turks • World Wars • Soviet rule • Striving for independence • After independence • Separatist movements • Transnistria separatists • Gagauz separatists • The future

31 GOVERNMENT
Constitutional division of power • Government institutions • National security • Political parties • Recent elections • International relations • Transnistrian conflict

41 ECONOMY
Change to market economy • Agriculture • Industry • Energy • Infrastructure • Public transportation • Measuring progress • Economic challenges

53 MOLDOVANS
Population trends • Where people live • The issue of ethnicity • Moldovan character • Local customs • Traditional dress

61 LIFESTYLE
Life events • The Moldovan family • Education • Health • Women's issues • Organized crime • Housing

73 RELIGION
Eastern Orthodox Church • Religion under Soviet rule • Orthodox view • Church architecture • The role of hymms • Monasteries

CONTENTS

83 LANGUAGE
Development of Moldovan • Language policy from 1812 to 1917 • Language in the Moldavian Socialist Soviet Republic • Use of Russian before independence • The media

91 ARTS
Cultural traditions • Folk culture • Painting • Church frescoes • Music • Monuments and statues • Theater • Literary traditions

101 LEISURE
Relaxing at home • Concerts and theater • Outdoor pursuits • Rural activities • Sports

107 FESTIVALS
New Year's Day • Easter • Christmas • Festival of the Transfiguration • Secular holidays • Traditional festivals

115 FOOD
A social occasion • Meal patterns • Daily meals • The Moldovan kitchen • Fresh produce • Traditional cuisine • Traditional drinks • Wine • Restaurants

122 MAP OF MOLDOVA

124 QUICK NOTES

125 GLOSSARY

126 BIBLIOGRAPHY

126 INDEX

A soldier takes a break from duty by playing music.

GEOGRAPHY

MOLDOVA IS A SMALL LANDLOCKED country approximately twice the size of Hawaii. Located between the Prut and Dniester rivers, it measures 217 miles (350 km) long and 93 miles (150 km) wide, covering around 13,047 square miles (33,800 square km). Moldova shares 279 miles (450 km) of border with Romania in the west and 583 miles (939 km) of border with Ukraine in the north, east, and south.

PHYSICAL ENVIRONMENT

Moldova is an extremely fertile land with an average elevation of 482 feet (147 m) above sea level. Its highest point, Mount Balanesti, stands at 1,407 feet (429 m). The country's topography is diverse, ranging gently from rolling, hilly plain in the north to deciduous forests and mountainous highlands in the center, to a steppe zone in the south.

Left: A village in Orhei district. One third of Moldova is covered by plains and fluvial terraces.

Opposite: A typical village in Moldova, with a church as a centerpiece.

RIVERS

There are approximately 3,000 rivers and streams in Moldova, and all of them drain south to the Black Sea. Only 246 exceed 6 miles (10 km) in length; eight extend more than 62 miles (100 km). Three river valleys running from northwest to southeast contain most of Moldova's towns. To the east, the Dniester forms part of the border with Ukraine and is navigable almost throughout the country. The Dniester drains an area of about 30,000 square miles (77,700 square km) and is an important traffic artery for the shipment of grain, vegetables, sunflower seeds, cattle and cattle products, and lumber. All these crops are produced in the Dniester basin. The Dniester swells during the rainy season and at the end of winter, when the ice starts to melt. If the winter is warm, however, the river does not freeze. The Raut, a short tributary of the Dniester, flows within a narrow valley in central Moldova. In the west, the Prut River divides Moldova from Romania. It is a tributary of the Danube, which it joins at the southern tip of the country. The Ialpug, Cogalnic, and other southern rivers flow into the estuary of the Danube River in nearby Ukraine.

There are 2,200 natural springs in Moldova. They are tapped for the country's water supply.

CLIMATE AND SEASONS

The country has a temperate continental climate. Average daily temperatures in the summer generally exceed 68°F (20°C). Winters are mild, with average daily temperatures ranging from 23°F to 27°F (-5°C to -3°C).

Conditions in the fall are changeable, with heavy rains in some years and droughts in others. Rain is heaviest in the higher regions, where it can exceed 23.6 inches (60 cm) per year. In the south, annual average precipitation is 13.8 inches (35 cm). In the past 110 years, 43 were drought years.

Opposite: **The Raut River on a hot summer afternoon.**

FLORA

About 1,800 plant species and an additional 3,000 species of moss, fungi, lichen, and algae can be found in Moldova. They grow primarily in the northern and eastern parts of the country. However, the various species are decreasing, and habitats for animals are becoming more scarce as a result of intensive land use and the destruction of wetlands.

Moldovan forests have the highest proportion of broad-leaved species of any temperate zone country. Oak trees are the predominant species, occupying 52% of total land area. The second most common species, Robinia, has been introduced to stabilize poor soils. It can survive in polluted soil and thus prevents erosion. Other indigenous species include ash, beech, and hornbeam. Forests of hornbeam used to be found in over one-third of Moldova, but now they can only be found in the central part of the country. In the Codri region forest types consist of broad-leaved tree species. Ash trees are found almost everywhere in the country, as are maple trees. Other flora include linden and wild pear.

FAUNA

Many different kinds of fauna flourish in Moldova. On the steppes, hamsters, hares, and partridges are predominant. The forest steppe is populated by animals such as wild boars, badgers, and wolves. The country has 15,000 animal species, 109 of which are endangered. Of all deer species, roe deer is the most common. Many other species of deer are no longer found in Moldova. To curb the declining numbers, some animal species have been introduced to the country. For example, the Kashmir deer was a local species that almost disappeared in the 1950s. Since then the Ascanian deer has been introduced to the Moldovan forests and reserves, as has the European elk and sika deer. Other imported species include the Siberian stag, fallow deer, and muskrat.

There are a rich variety of birds, both resident and migratory. Common species found include the hawk, wood lark, and long-eared owl. Along the rivers, ducks, wild geese, and herons can be seen.

Like animals, the dwindling fish population is of great concern to environmentalists. Among the 75 species, the most common are perch, pike, bream, and roach. Some species, such as trout, are no longer found in Moldova.

ENVIRONMENTAL ISSUES

SOIL POLLUTION During the last half of the 20th century, Moldova's agricultural land was heavily worked to produce cheap goods for the Soviet Union. Creation of new agricultural lands, careless cultivation, and contamination has led to soil degradation.

The greatest pollution comes from excessive fertilization: usage increased from 24 pounds (11 kg) per acre in 1965 to 178 pounds (80 kg) per acre in 1989. By 1990, 25% of the food produced was polluted with nitrates. Greater efforts are now being made to reduce this dependence on agricultural chemicals, but pesticide usage to improve yields will not stop overnight.

Some of the most severe cases of soil pollution take place in river valleys, such as in the Raut Valley, below.

In April 1999, 1.6 million trees and bushes were planted. Areas affected by landslides were primary targets. The operation, called "Green Day" action, has been in operation for the past five years.

CONSERVATION EFFORTS

Moldova has started a project to conserve its biovariety, supported by a $125,000 grant from the World Bank. The conservation project, with a coordinating council of 70 experts, aims to preserve Moldova's flora and fauna and make people aware of the country's biological resources. Total plant and animal species are decreasing, and some plant species risk extinction in Moldova as they are less protected by the state, compared to conservation efforts in other European countries. In the last quarter of the 20th century, no natural seed reproduction occurred, and the place of the disappeared plants was taken by all kinds of weeds, such as nettle, catchweed, and bedstraw.

The only nature conservation is found in the reserved areas. By 1989, two zoological and nine botanical sanctuaries or partially reserved areas, called *zakazinki* ("ZA-GA-zinc-kee"), were built. Conservation areas include the Codri State Zapovedniki (close to the highest peak), the Yagorlyk Zapovednik, and the Redensky Les Hunting Preserve. Exclusive control over natural resource administration and nature preservation lies with the State Department for Environment and Natural Resource Protection, which was formed in 1990.

WATER POLLUTION About 1.3 million people depend on surface water in Moldova, while the rest of the population consumes underground water. Eight percent of the water comes from aquifers, and only half of the water meets drinking standards. Many of the rural wells are either drying up or are contaminated with minerals and bacteria. Most of the river valleys and lake areas are in use for agricultural production, and Moldova has no system to remove chemicals and salt from the polluted water. Moldova also lacks almost any source of chemically cleaned drinking water that is within the admissible standards of hygiene.

AIR POLLUTION Under the Soviets, pollution controls were not installed, and emissions from factories in neighboring republics drifted over Moldova. Today, polluted air is mostly found in Balti, Rabnita, Chisinau, and Tiraspol, and three-quarters of it is caused by cars. High formalde-hyde concentrations have been discovered in Balti and Chisinau, where levels have reached four times the maximum permissible concentration. Since the Chernobyl disaster in 1986, local power plants have stepped up their vigilance. Radioactive waste was buried in this region, and a few accidents in the past have added to the contamination.

CITIES

Moldova has 21 cities and towns, 48 city-type settlements, and more than 1,600 villages. The major cities include the capital city, Chisinau (formerly spelled Kishinev), with 735,000 people; Tiraspol, with 204,000; Balti, with 157,000; and Tighina, with 137,000.

CHISINAU Founded in 1420, Chisinau lies on the Ikel River in the center of Moldova. It grew rapidly from a small village into an important rail junction between Romania and Russia during the 19th century. Chisinau suffered massive destruction during World War II, when bombing and fighting destroyed more than 70% of the buildings. Most of the existing buildings date from the mid-20th century when the city was rebuilt. Main streets were widened, tall office buildings were constructed, and new industrial parks were planned. Factories in the suburbs account for nearly half of all industrial production in Moldova. Many shops are found in the capital, as shopping is a major recreational pursuit. The city looks like a

The Cioflea Church—a landmark building in Chisinau.

typical Soviet provincial city—built on a rectangular grid with huge concrete, nondescript buildings. Along the main street, the monotony is broken with some Neoclassical mansions—a reminder of the country's past. Since independence, the main street has been renamed Boulevard Stefan cel Mare instead of Lenina after Lenin. Many other streets have also been renamed, in most instances, to honor Romanians instead of Soviet figures. Piata Nationala, the main square, has a truimphal arch built in 1846. Behind it is a huge cathedral recently restored and a park with a section reserved for statues from the classics of Romanian literature.

The city is the center of arts in the country. It has numerous museums, such as the National Art Museum, the National History Museum, and the Archaeology Museum, theaters, and an opera house. A beautiful lake runs along the central park of the city, which is located near the state university. One of the city's most beautiful buildings is the Cioflea Church. It has majestic, sky-blue towers, and the icons inside the church are each decorated with a different frame.

TIRASPOL, the second largest city in Moldova, is located east of Tighina on the Dniester River. Tiraspol was founded in 1792. Like other cities, it faced heavy destruction during battles between the Soviet Union and Germany. Today it is the capital of the self-proclaimed republic, Transnistria. Its population consists of mainly Russians, ethnic Moldovans, and ethnic Ukrainians.

Tiraspol is now an industrial center well known for canning and wine making. Other industries in Tiraspol produce farm equipment, footwear, textiles, furniture, and carpets.

BALTI lies on the Raut River and is the largest city in the north. It is home to several of Moldova's major industries, such as wine making, sugar refining, and tobacco processing. Fur coats, machinery, and furniture are also manufactured.

A statue of Suvorov, a hero who fought the Ottoman Turks in the 16th century.

TIGHINA is one of the country's oldest cities, founded around the second century B.C. Its Russian name is Bender, which means "belonging to the Turks." Tighina is situated southeast of Chisinau on the Dniester River. Throughout history, the city has been attacked and occupied by different foreign powers. It has also been rebuilt many times following destruction in various violent clashes. In 1992 it was again the center of fighting between ethnic Russians and the Moldovan military. Today it is the place where Russian-led peacekeeping forces in the region live.

Tighina is a manufacturing center for textiles, electrical equipment, and food. Silk made in Tighina is among the finest in the world. A 17th-century Turkish fortress still stands in the city as a reminder of the turbulent past.

HISTORY

THROUGHOUT HISTORY, Moldova has been subject to frequent invasions and foreign domination. Each group left a legacy, but Moldova has been mostly influenced by the Soviet Union. The imperial and Soviet governments tried to integrate Moldova's economy into their own and Russianize the Moldovan people. For a long time this plan seemed to work, but in 1991 Moldova declared independence and went its separate way. Independence was not a new experience for the country, as it had existed briefly as a sovereign state before, but this time there was much to undo from the previous regime.

Above: **Transnistrian people asking for Russian support in a demonstration.**

Opposite: **A young volunteer soldier on the lookout for outbreaks of violence.**

EARLY HISTORY

The Dacians were the ancestors of the Moldovans. Numerous archeological traces have been found, including burial places and religious cult constructions between the Dniester and the Prut rivers, dating to the fourth century B.C.. The Dacians were farmers who settled in the river valleys. They traded with the Greeks, who had established trading posts along the Black Sea coast.

The Romans conquered the Dacians in the second and third centuries A.D., and the local population had to learn Latin. The Romans built roads, forts, and trading centers but eventually left the area for conquests farther afield. Slavs settled in their wake. About this time the Romanian language developed from Latin. Various nobles ruled the area, and one of them, called Bogdan, founded the principality of Moldavia, which included the area known as Bessarabia (modern Moldova). The first document referring to the land of Moldavia dates to A.D. 1360. In 1391 ethnic Moldavians were mentioned for the first time.

A monument to Stephen the Great, hero in the hearts of many Moldovans. About 1,000 streets are named after him in Moldova and Romania.

MOLDAVIA AND THE TURKS

The most important figure to the formation of the medieval Moldavian state was Stephen the Great (1457–1504), who defended Moldovia's sovereignty in battles with the Turks, Hungarians, Polish royal troops, and the Crimean Khans. Fortresses from his time still stand. The medieval principality was, for much of its history, under Austro-Hungarian rule. A large part of Moldavia was later incorporated into present-day Romania and Ukraine.

During his rule, Stephen organized a great, strong force of peasants to resist the Turkish sultan. His efforts were successful until 1503, when he finally signed a treaty with the sultan that managed to preserve Moldavia's independence. During his lifetime he was a supporter of the arts and a religious crusader, and his architects built Orthodox churches throughout the country. Stephen also increased trade links with Europe and the Middle East.

In 1513 Moldavia became part of the Turkish Empire and remained so for the next 300 years. This was a stable period, but by the 18th century, the empire began to break up. Between 1711 and 1812, the Russians gained control of Moldavia five times. Eventually Turkey was defeated by Russia. As a result of the Treaty of Bucharest in 1812, which ended the Russian-Turkish war, Moldavia became part of the Russian Empire. But this did not last very long. By the beginning of the 20th century, western Moldavia had become part of the united nation of Romania. Bessarabia, in the eastern part of Moldavia, remained under Russian control.

WORLD WARS

During World War I, Russia suffered great damage. There were widespread food shortages, and people became disillusioned with the empire. Following the Bolshevik Revolution in 1917, the Russian Empire collapsed, a year before the war ended. Bessarabia declared independence from Russia and united with Romania. A treaty was signed October 20, 1920.

In 1922 the Russian communist leaders founded the Union of Soviet Socialist Republics (USSR), which included Russia, Ukraine, and several nearby republics. In 1939 the USSR, led by Stalin, and Germany, led by Hitler, signed a treaty that banned hostilities between the two countries and allowed Stalin to annex territory. A year later, the USSR occupied Bessarabia and renamed it the Moldavian Soviet Socialist Republic.

When World War II began, the USSR had to defend itself against Hitler, despite their nonaggression pact. Romania, allied with Germany, attacked Ukraine and briefly reoccupied Soviet Moldavia from 1941 to 1944 until Soviet forces again retook the territory.

SOVIET RULE

With the restoration of Soviet rule in 1944, Moldavia was subjected to large-scale immigration of Russians and Ukrainians, especially to the industrial centers along the eastern bank of the Dniester. Stalin decided that Moldavians and Romanians were now separate ethnic groups, even though the former had relatives across the Prut River in Romania. He insisted that the language they spoke was not Romanian but Moldavian, and imposed the Cyrillic alphabet used by Russians to replace the Latin alphabet used by Romanians. Russian became the official language.

In 1950 Leonid Brezhnev, a Soviet official from Ukraine, was sent to Moldavia to ensure compliance with Soviet laws. Private farms were declared Soviet property, and government-run farms were worked under the direction of Russian and Ukrainian managers. During the 1970s and 1980s, after becoming president of the USSR, Brezhnev continued the policy of Russianization. The Soviet government closed churches and synagogues, and more ethnic Russians and Ukrainians settled in Moldavia.

STRIVING FOR INDEPENDENCE

Moldova's gradual movement to independence sped up in 1986 with Mikhail Gorbachev's reformist regime and policy of *glasnost* ("GLASS-nos"), which means "openness." Gorbachev was the new president of the USSR. As the Soviet Union started to relax its policies, a number of independent political groups in Moldova evolved, working toward national and cultural independence. The Popular Front of Moldavia was formed, and proindependence pressure, often supported by mass demonstrations, intensified.

The leaders of Soviet Moldavia agreed to some demands, such as the use of the Latin alphabet, and Romanian names replaced Russian names for major cities. Moldova's progress toward independence and reform accelerated after an economist, Mircea Druc, was appointed prime minister in May 1990. In June 1990 the Moldavian parliament changed the republic's name to Moldova, adopted the blue, yellow, and red colors of Romania's flag, and issued a declaration of sovereignty. The following summer, 100,000 Moldovans took to the streets demanding independence, and Gorbachev could do little to stop Moldova from leaving the Soviet Union.

AFTER INDEPENDENCE

On August 27, 1991, the Republic of Moldova officially gained its independence and became a sovereign state. The move was followed by the establishment of customs posts on the border with Ukraine. A Moldovan national army was also formed.

The first presidential elections were held in December 1991, in which a Moldovan, Mircea Snegur, was elected president. Multiparty parliamentary elections were held in February 1994, and the Communist-led Agrarian Democratic Party won the largest number of seats. A bloc of socialist parties came in second. Petru C. Lucinschi was elected speaker of the parliament, and the government was headed by Prime Minister Andrei Sangheli. The parliament passed a new constitution for the Republic of Moldova, and April 1995 saw the first multiparty elections held for local, self-governing bodies. Presidential elections were held in 1996.

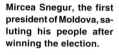

Mircea Snegur, the first president of Moldova, saluting his people after winning the election.

SEPARATIST MOVEMENTS

The single most important political challenge facing Moldova after gaining independence was resistance to Moldovan rule and separatism by two ethnic minorities. The first group lives on the eastern side of the Dniester, in a region known as Transnistria, and is led by ethnic Russians. The second group, in the south of the country, is led by members of the Gagauz ("ga-GA-ooze"), a Christian, Turkic ethnic group.

When Moldova became independent, these two groups were concerned about their future and about the protection of their national and ethnic status in the new republic. These concerns were based on fears that Moldova would unite with Romania, as regions of Moldova had historically been part of Romania. These fears were exacerbated when Moldovan became the official language of Moldova, although Russian was permitted for interethnic communication. Russian speakers marched through the capital and walked off their jobs to protest what they viewed as increased discrimination. Their displeasure remains today.

TRANSNISTRIA SEPARATISTS

Tensions between ethnic Romanians and ethnic Russians worsened in 1990. Local officials refused to enact the language law in the area east of the Dniester, where large numbers of Slavs reside but do not constitute a majority of the population. A political group promoting greater autonomy for the area was formed. On September 2, 1990, Transnistria separatists declared an Autonomous Soviet Socialist Republic, which the Moldovan parliament immediately annulled. Violence erupted in November 1990 during elections for representatives to the Transnistria Supreme Soviet. The conflict escalated in late 1991 when, following Moldova's declaration of independence from the Soviet Union, the leaders of the Transnistria separatists declared the region's independence from Moldova. Fighting erupted and escalated in the spring of 1992, resulting in many lives lost and considerable damage to the economies of both Transnistria and Moldova.

A ceasefire was declared in July 1992, and the Russian 14th Army, based in the Transnistrian region prior to Moldovan independence, acted as peacekeepers. To prevent further bloodshed, the Moldovan and Russian prime ministers later signed a withdrawal treaty.

In 1995 the Russian president, Boris Yeltsin, acknowledged Moldova's territorial integrity, and the issue of Transnistria's sovereignty returned to the negotiating table. A signed accord guaranteed Transnistria's autonomy, but independence was not granted. Nevertheless, Transnistria took matters into its own hands and held elections in December 1995, much to the displeasure of the Moldovan government. Igor Smirnov was elected president of the region.

In May 1997 a memorandum recognizing Moldova's territorial integrity over Transnistria was signed in Moscow. Discussions commenced for the drafting of a final document to govern the normalization of relations between Moldova and the Transnistria separatists. President Yeltsin has indicated that Russian troops would stay in the region until a settlement is reached.

Above: **A soldier stationed at Tighina.**

Opposite: **Family members grieving over the loss of their loved one after fighting broke out between the Transnistrian separatists and Moldovan soldiers.**

GAGAUZ SEPARATISTS

A Christian Turkic minority, the Gagauz enjoy local autonomy in the southern part of the country. In August 1990 the Gagauz proclaimed an Autonomous Soviet Socialist Republic, which the Moldovan parliament did not recognize. The 1994 Moldovan elections marked the turning point in relations between the Moldovan government and Gagauz representatives. One particularly important issue for the Gagauz was the abolition of the 1989 language law, which made Moldovan the only official language. As the majority of the Gaugaz are not fluent in Moldovan, they are afraid that they will lose their influence in the country.

A new law has since designated Moldovan, Gagauzian, and Russian as the three official languages. The Moldovan parliament also ratified the Gagauz region's special status. Under Moldovan law, the Gagauz region remains part of Moldovan territory, and the Moldovan government determines its budget. A locally elected parliamentary assembly, governor, and executive committee act as the local government. In elections for the executive committee and parliamentary assembly, held in the spring and summer of 1995, the Communist Party gained the largest number of seats.

THE FUTURE

In 1992 Moldova joined the Commonwealth of Independent States (CIS), an alliance of former Soviet republics, and gained a seat in the United Nations. The alliance with CIS helped Moldova acquire raw materials and provide a market for its finished goods, which is necessary now that the Soviet Union has ceased to exist. There is constant tension between conservatives in the country who want to return to the old days of central control and liberals who want a restructured market economy. The strained relations between Moldovans and ethnic Russians and Turks in their autonomous areas continues, and while Russian troops remain in Transnistria, this will remain a serious issue.

Opposite: **Grigori Tabunscic, the president of Gagauz.**

Below: **A soldier belonging to the united peace corps on Tighina Bridge. The peace corps include Russian, Ukrainian, and Moldovan troops.**

GOVERNMENT

MOLDOVA HAS WORKED HARD to establish democratic political systems, but changing from a communist
government to a real democracy is difficult. The task is
complicated by many who view democracy as chaotic
and unstable, and they yearn for the predictability of the
old days and the privileges they had enjoyed.

A presidency, universal suffrage, and popular elections
have been added to the basic Soviet government structure.
However, the country's first attempt at democracy resulted
in the Communist Party winning a majority of seats in the
parliament, which made legislative compromises among
the various ethnic groups impossible. A smaller parliament
and a larger number of moderates after the 1994 elections have made
legislative progress easier.

CONSTITUTIONAL DIVISION OF POWER

The new constitution of Moldova, passed by the national parliament on
July 29, 1994, defines Moldova as a sovereign state with a free market
economy based on protection of private property rights and independent
executive, legislative, and judicial branches of government.

Personal rights and freedoms are ensured according to the UN
Universal Declaration of Human Rights. All citizens are equal before the
law, regardless of ethnicity, language, religion, or political beliefs. The
state guarantees the rights of political parties and other public organizations. In keeping with its ethnic and cultural diversity, the constitution
enshrines the rights of all minorities and the autonomous status of the
Transnistria and Gagauz regions. Administration of the cities and municipali-
ties is based on the principles of local autonomy and democratic elections.

GOVERNMENT INSTITUTIONS

THE EXECUTIVE BRANCH consists of the president and the government of Moldova. The president is elected in a national election for a term of four years. He has broad powers and acts as the head of state and the head of the military, with authority to declare states of military emergency, subject to parliamentary approval.

The president appoints a prime minister, with the consent of parliament. He leads a Council of Ministers that carries out the functions of government. The president must be over 35 years old, a resident in Moldova for at least 10 years, and a speaker of the state language.

THE LEGISLATIVE BRANCH consists of a directly elected parliament. The parliament's 104 members are elected from party lists on a proportional representation basis. Parliament sits for four years and has the power to adopt laws, approve the state budget, determine military matters, and exercise certain supervisory powers over the work of the government.

JUDICIAL BRANCH Moldova possesses a three-tier judicial system that is independent of the executive and legislative branches. Municipal and district courts are generally courts of first instance, with appeals first to an appellate court and then ultimately to the Supreme Court, the highest court in Moldova. There are also specialized courts with jurisdiction over economic and military disputes. A constitutional court, which is independent of other courts, has jurisdiction over all matters relating to the interpretation of the provisions of the Moldovan constitution. Judges for the lower courts are appointed by the president for an initial period of five years. They may be reappointed for a subsequent 10 years. Supreme Court judges are appointed by parliament for terms of not less than 15 years.

NATIONAL SECURITY

Armed forces are under the jurisdiction of the Ministry of Defense. In 1995 ground forces totaled about 11,000 and air force personnel, about 1,300. There are 100,000 reservists, those who had military service in the previous five years. Military units for the army consist of three motor rifle brigades, one artillery brigade, and one reconnaissance or assault battalion. The air force has one fighter regiment, one helicopter squadron, and one missile brigade. Military equipment includes arms from former Soviet stocks and undetermined quantities of arms from Romania. Internal security is provided by 2,500 national policemen and a riot police force of 900 under the Ministry of Interior. The Russian 14th Army, acting as peacekeepers in Moldova, has a total force of 14,200. Guarding the Transnistrian region are the "Cossacks," the armed forces of the self-proclaimed republic.

Moldovan troops standing at attention. The universal conscription for army reserves is up to 18 months.

POLITICAL PARTIES

One of the main political parties in Moldova is the Agrarian Democratic Party (DAP), led by former Communists and those favoring closer economic links with the CIS. Their supporters include the rural people, economic conservatives, and ethnic minorities who oppose reunification with Romania.

Another main party is the Christian Democratic Popular Front, which supports reintegration of Moldova into Romania. It was formerly a faction of the Moldavian Popular Front, which was the strongest political party in the capital and the areas populated by ethnic Romanians. The Popular Front fell apart as a result of internal disputes.

A union of leftist, left-centrist, and centrist parties was set up in June 1998. Members of this ULLCCP political bloc are the Communist Party, Agrarian Democratic Party, Party of Socialists, Socialist Party, Femeia Moldovei (Moldova's Women), Alliance of Democratic Youth, and Centrist-Democratic Rebirth Party.

The main parties in Transnistria are the Bloc of Patriotic Forces, which opposes rapprochement with Moldova, and the more moderate Movement for the Development of Dniester. One party in Gagauz is the Gagauz People.

RECENT ELECTIONS

Petru Lucinschi was elected in the presidential election held in December 1996. During his office, his government has survived many votes of no confidence. There has been a lot of political bickering and internal dissension. Leaders lack the political will to give up traditional bases of power and deal with the massive problems in the country. In early 1999 Premier Ion Ciubuc, disappointed with the stagnant political situation in his country, finally announced his resignation, and the government collapsed. President Lucinschi believed a new government would be formed within 10 to 14 days after he appointed Ion Sturza as prime minister and Sturza chose his cabinet. However, his nominations were rejected by parliament, and there was a crisis for many months. Finally in March 1999, after a long period of uncertainty that left Moldova without an effective government, a new cabinet proposed by Sturza was approved by parliament. The new cabinet has members that represent 20 ministries.

Below: **Mircea Snegur, the first president of Moldova, congratulates Petru Lucinschi on his victory in the presidential election.**

Opposite: **Vasile Nedelciuc, a deputy in parliament. He belongs to the Democratic Forces Party.**

INTERNATIONAL RELATIONS

Since Moldova gained independence on August 27, 1991, many foreign countries have officially recognized its status. This is a very encouraging sign for the infant nation. At present, Moldova maintains diplomatic relations with 109 countries. Moldova is also a member of a number of multilateral organizations—the European Bank for Reconstruction and Development, the International Bank for Reconstruction and Development or World Bank, and the International Monetary Fund (IMF). In November 1994 the European Union (EU) and the Moldovan government signed a partnership and cooperation agreement, and in July 1995 Moldova was admitted to the Council of Europe.

Belarussian President Alexander Lukashenko (center) receives the traditional welcome gift of bread and salt as his Moldovan counterpart Petru Lucinschi looks on.

Moldova is a member of the United Nations. Discussions were initiated in 1992 between the Moldovan government and the UN Development Program (UNDP). With UNDP's assistance, programs in democracy, the promotion of entrepreneurial activity, women in development, foreign trade, disaster mitigation, and sustainable human development were efficiently initiated.

In early 1993 Moldova signed the Paris Charter of the Conference on Security and Cooperation in Europe, now called the OSCE. Moldova is also a member of the NATO Partnership for Peace program.

Moldova and other former Soviet republics form the Commonwealth of Independent States (CIS), which promotes cooperation among its members. In September 1993 an agreement establishing an Economic Union was signed by all CIS countries, including Moldova. In addition, the country has entered into agreements on the creation of a free trade zone and payment union with Russia and a number of other CIS countries.

Moldovan Foreign Minister Nicolae Tabacaru is considering the possibility of joining the European Union, an economic and political union of the major European countries. Tabacaru believes that Moldova must first achieve economic stability before applying for membership. This means that Moldova may join the European Union only in the beginning of the third millennium.

RELATIONS WITH IMMEDIATE NEIGHBORS

Relations with Romania have been excellent in recent years, and many Moldovans wish for the reunification of these two countries, since they are so closely related. Ukraine has looked more favorably on Moldova lately as Moldova has adopted less nationalistic policies. The relationship with Russia is still very tense, and the continued presence of the Russian 14th Army in Transnistria is seen as a common threat.

Russian soldiers keeping the peace in Tiraspol.

TRANSNISTRIAN CONFLICT

Moldova remains divided, with Slavic separatists controlling Transnistria along the Ukranian border. This separatist regime has entered negotiations with the national government on the possibility of a special status for the region. Despite the signing of a memorandum on the basis for normalizing relations, progress has been blocked by the separatists' continuing demands for "statehood" and recognition of Moldova as a confederation of two equal states. The Organization for Security and Cooperation in Europe, the Russian Federation, and Ukraine act as mediators. The two sides have generally observed the ceasefire of July 1992, but other agreements to normalize relations have not always been honored.

Mediators in the Transnistrian settlement negotiations representing Russia and Ukraine drafted an agreement in 1999 that recognizes Moldova as an independent, sovereign state and defines Transnistria as an autonomous republic within the Republic of Moldova. According to the draft agreement, Transnistria would have its own state symbols—flag, emblem, anthem—and three official languages, namely Moldovan, Ukrainian, and Russian. The mediators urged all sides to continue the peacekeeping operations in Transnistria with the added participation of Ukrainian peacekeepers.

A negotiated resolution to this conflict has been in progress since 1995, but it is only recently that the meetings have become constructive and a level of understanding has developed. Both sides have realized that without a solution to the status of Transnistria, all economic and social problems will be extremely difficult to solve.

PRESIDENT PETRU LUCINSCHI

President Lucinschi was born January 27, 1940, in a village in northern Moldova. He graduated from the Moldova State University with a Ph.D. in history and was the executive director of the Foundation of Social Sciences in Moscow and a senior fellow at the Institute of Social and Political Studies in Moscow.

Before Moldova gained its independence in 1991, Lucinschi was the first secretary of the Moldovan Communist Party Central Committee and a member of the Communist Party of the Soviet Union (CPSU) Central Committee. In 1971–1989 he held senior positions in various Soviet Union state bodies in Moldova, Tajikistan, and Moscow, including deputy head of the Propaganda Department of the CPSU Central Committee, secretary of the Central Committee of the Tajikistan Communist Party, and the head of the Moldovan Komsomol (Young Communist League). By 1992 he was the Ambassador of the Republic of Moldova to the Russian Federation. In 1994 he became the speaker of parliament.

Petru Lucinschi was elected president December 1, 1996. He defeated incumbent Mircea Snegur with 54.07% of the popular vote. Lucinschi ran as an independent on a platform of socially oriented reforms, democracy, and national unity and was supported by the Socialist Party, the Communist Party, and the ruling Agrarian Democratic Party. He is married with children and his favorite saying is, "A clever man always gets out of trouble, while a wise one never gets into it." His favorite joke? "Can one buy an honest person?"—"No, an honest person can only be sold."

Peacekeeping troops in Transnistria consist of 14,200 Russians equipped with 26 tanks and 90 armored vehicles, and peacekeepers, which include 498 Moldovans, 459 Russians, and about 500 Transnistrians. The Organization for Security and Cooperation in Europe periodically reviews the situation in Transnistria. It stresses that cooperation on all sides is necessary to reduce the arms and ammunition that have been building up in Transnistria since the conflict began in 1991. Several participating states are willing to contribute either financially or with technical assistance to this project.

ECONOMY

MOLDOVA'S RESOURCES ARE SUFFICIENT to secure economic independence and provide an adequate standard of living for its people. Relatively inexpensive labor, a strategic location, good infrastructure, and developed telecommunications are distinct competitive advantages. One limiting factor is its reliance on imported energy supplies. The transition from a system of central, government control to a market economy is painful, and vested interests have sought to maintain the old system or, at least, to make large profits during the transition.

Despite these obstacles, strict economic policies have continued, allowing the country to reap the benefits of decreasing inflation, a stable currency, and a shrinking budget deficit. In the early 1990s Moldova was in the group of industrially developed countries. This is good news indeed for its hardworking people.

CHANGE TO MARKET ECONOMY

Before independence, Moldova specialized in agricultural products and consumer goods and relied on other republics for raw materials. Russia supplied heavily subsidized fuel, and this made Moldova's goods inexpensive and affordable to the other Soviet republics. After the breakup of the Soviet Union in 1991, energy shortages led to sharp production declines. Improving the efficiency of their industries became paramount, and the steps taken toward improving efficiency from 1991 to 1994 included privatization, or the sale of former state-owned property, and changing laws to make businesses more compatible with a free market and foreign investment.

Above: **A penniless Moldovan woman begging for money.**

Opposite: **Growing grapes is one of the most profitable business ventures in Moldova.**

AGRICULTURE

Moldova has a favorable climate and good farmland—thus the economy depends heavily on agriculture. Some 86% of the land is used for agriculture. The agricultural sector employs about 700,000 people. Crops, primarily fruit and berries, grain, grapes, tobacco, vegetables, sugar beets, potatoes, and sunflowers, have traditionally accounted for the biggest share of agricultural production. Unfortunately, a succession of natural disasters in recent years—drought, frosts, and floods—has taken a toll.

The most radical change, however, has been the gradual ending of state collective farming and the introduction of privately owned land with individual responsibility for the costs of production. State and collective farms have been transformed into joint-stock companies, and by the end of 1999, the amount of agricultural land privatized was 90%. Financial and technical assistance from Western governments, substantial government subsidies, and tax incentives are now being employed to ease the burden of farmers.

Moldova's agriculture minister has described the year 1998 as the most difficult for Moldovan farming in the past 40 years. The total agricultural output in 1998 was only 89% of the 1997 figures. Difficulties were caused by the Russian financial crisis, the privatization of farm equipment, and confusing agricultural policies. The sugar, tobacco, wine, and canning industries reduced their production because of a shortage of raw materials. At the same time, 4,942 acres (2,000 hectares) of sugarbeets went unharvested, and 40% of the fruit crop planned for 1998 was destroyed by a lack of chemicals and funds. Fruit producers ended the year with huge losses. Most of the fruit harvested was of poor quality and had to be sold to processing enterprises at low prices.

Cattle, hogs, poultry, and lambs are raised, but livestock numbers have continued to fall since the drought in 1994. Rising costs have resulted in high consumer prices and a fall in local consumption.

Before the break-up of the Soviet Union, Moldova rated sixth in food production among the 15 former Soviet republics.

Children tending cattle.

43

Workers in the finishing department of a pump factory.

INDUSTRY

There are about 600 large-scale and midsized enterprises, which account for about one-third of the gross domestic product and 300,000 jobs.

The processing of fruit and vegetables is done by seven large enterprises, 15 medium-sized units, and 100 small facilities. Field tomatoes and apples account for 80% of all processed output. The remaining 20% of output includes canned goods, dehydrated fruits, purees for baby food, jams and preserves, and some specialty products. Almost all the fruit and vegetables are harvested by hand, resulting in products with better flavor, texture, and appearance than mechanically harvested crops.

Sugarbeets are an important crop with excellent prospects. About 1.8 million tons of sugarbeets are processed into 230,000 tons of white sugar each year. In contrast to other products, sugar exports increased substantially from 1991 to 1994. A persistent shortage of refined sugar in the Commonwealth of Independent States (CIS) ensures a steady demand for sugar and thus secures the future of Moldovan sugar producers.

MAIN INDUSTRIES

Food processing – 46.2%
Electric energy – 17.7%
Engineering and metal processing – 10.8%
Light industry – 6.2%
Construction materials – 4.5%
Forestry, wood processing, pulp, and paper – 4.3%
Glass making – 2.1%
Chemicals – 0.6%
Other – 7.6%

The furniture-making and wood processing industry includes 27 enterprises that produce contemporary furniture. The furniture is popular both domestically and abroad.

The tobacco industry consists of eight fermentation plants and the Chisinau tobacco factory, which can produce a massive amount of 9.1 billion cigarettes a year.

More than 50 engineering plants produce high-tech equipment, including electronics, automation and telecommunications equipment, television sets, electric engines, pumps, tractors and other agricultural machinery, refrigerators, and other appliances. The light industry sector consists of 56 enterprises. They manufacture carpets, textiles, garments, and footwear.

There are 150 wineries in Moldova. The country's wines are becoming more well known in Europe and the United States and are of a higher quality than wines in the same price range from neighboring countries. In a competition in 1993 in Bordeaux, Moldovan dry wines won all the prizes, except the Grand Prix. Anti-alcohol campaigns in the USSR in Gorbachev's time had a devastating effect on the industry, and Moldovan viticulture received no investment between 1985 and 1992, so the need for modern equipment and marketing is now acute. Investment in the industry is likely to increase further once viticulturists gain control of the actual vineyard land and not just the wineries. Although farmers are opposed to this move, the wine industry is pressing for rapid reforms.

Tourism is a developing industry, and investments allow the development of facilities for tourists at local archeological, architectural, and cultural landmarks, such as the monastery of Capriana and the fortresses of Soroca and Tighina.

ENERGY

The nucleus of the national energy system is a thermal power plant. It has a capacity of 2.5 million kilowatts. Moldova is currently seeking alternative energy sources and is working to develop its own energy supplies, such as solar power, wind, and geothermal. The country is also implementing a national energy conservation program.

Energy efficiency is a priority on the government's agenda, as Moldova depends almost entirely on Russia for its oil, gasoline, coal, and natural gas to fuel power generation plants. As supplies become both expensive and scarce, the government has to carefully ration domestic and industrial energy consumption. Many industries are badly affected as a result of the lack of energy.

INFRASTRUCTURE

The infrastucture of Moldova is quite developed. Its road network is over 6,210 miles (10,000 km) long, of which slightly more than 1,863 miles (3,000 km) are important highways, and the rest are local roads. Only 62% of the total road length has an improved asphalt pavement. Automobiles, buses, and trucks transport 96% of cargo and 85% of passengers.

As an agricultural country, Moldova depends on a reliable transportation network to ensure the efficient domestic movement of produce and the export of agricultural goods. Railroads transport 95% of exports. The rail system extends for 818 miles (1,318 km). Air transportation is represented by Air Moldova, a state company, as well as Moldavian Airlines and Air Moldova International, two commercial air carriers. A project providing for the reconstruction and modernization of the Chisinau international air terminal is underway. Four airfields support international and domestic travel. The Dniester River is used for ferrying tourists and local cargo. The construction of a port and fuel terminal is scheduled at the meeting point of the Prut and the Danube to serve tankers and other ships.

Below: **A crew from Air Moldova. Direct flights are available to and from Frankfurt, Vienna, Budapest, Athens, Tel Aviv, Paris, Istanbul, Warsaw, Bucharest, Moscow, and other CIS cities.**

Opposite: **A high voltage line of electrotransfers, component parts of a power grid.**

PUBLIC TRANSPORTATION

Three electric trolley parks in Chisinau operate 240 trolleys. In addition, buses run from 5 a.m. to midnight at regular intervals, and taxis are available. Moldova's highways are mainly two-lane roads, unevenly maintained and unlighted.

In 1998 Chisinau's trolleys carried a total of 280 million passengers. Forty-seven groups of Moldovans, including pensioners, students, Afghan war veterans, invalids, police officers, and fire-fighters, have the right to use public transportation free of charge. Approximately 80% of all passengers ride free. The city has no plans to raise ticket prices in the near future. The transportation company is worried that if they do, many people will stop using the trolleys altogether, and others will just switch to private taxis and minibuses.

MEASURING PROGRESS

During the transition years of 1991 to 1994, Moldova's GDP declined in most sectors—industry, agriculture, construction, and transportation. Inflation slowed in 1994 as a result of a tighter monetary policy.

Moldova's trade deficit can be attributed to a lack of energy resources and increases in energy prices, the lack of an external marketing network for Moldovan products, and the decline of production. Much depends on how successful the export of wine, canned fruits, and other agricultural products becomes.

The CIS takes 61% of Moldova's exports and provides 67% of imports. After Russia, Ukraine, and Belarus, Uzbekistan is Moldova's fourth most important trade partner. The US market remains unknown to Moldova, but as this market opens up, opportunities are presenting themselves to local entrepreneurs.

The national currency, the Moldovan leu (plural: lei), was introduced in November 1993, initially set at lei 3.85 to one US dollar. The exchange rate of the Moldovan leu has demonstrated greater stability through the 1990s than the currencies of neighboring countries, including Russia, Romania, and Ukraine. To the Moldovans, this is encouraging.

PRIVATIZATION

The first stage of the privatization program was in 1993–95 and involved about 1,600 enterprises or 40–50% of state assets. Agricultural privatization meant the transfer of shares of some state and collective farms to present and former farm employees. At least 10% of state holdings in agriculture were transferred to private owners in 1992, and further sales took place in 1993. Agricultural processing enterprises were converted into joint-stock companies with 50% share distribution to suppliers, 20% to employees, and 30% to the Ministry of Privatization. Privatized land will not be tradable until January 2001. Some state corporations were designated to remain in state ownership, including some utilities, scientific institutes, and large-scale food processing companies. Little progress was made until the middle of 1994. By June 1995 the private sector accounted for 48% of industrial production, 81% of major construction projects, 55% of passenger transportation, and 41% of the retail and trade sector. The first stage was completed in December 1995, when the last of 1,132 large enterprises and 613 shops were sold and the auctions closed. Two-thirds of the country's non-agricultural economy had been transferred to the private sector, in what has been described as one of the most far-reaching—and fastest—privatization initiatives.

The second phase of privatization was to attract foreign direct investment. The 1995–96 privatization program scheduled another 1,450 enterprises for privatization. Of this number, 280 medium-sized companies, covering 30% of the initial state assets in the economic sector, were transferred to private ownership. The priorities included agricultural processing, utilities, transportation, railways, and telecommunications. Some 804 of the firms were privatized for vouchers, 183 for cash, and the remainder for a combination of vouchers and cash. By January 1, 1996, about 2,278 enterprises had been privatized. During the process, 3,200 plots of land owned by fruit-growing associations were sold for cash. In total, 190,200 apartments were privatized, accounting for 80.7% of the total housing owned by the state.

By 1998 the number of privatized enterprises had increased 1.5-fold in Moldova. The US Agency for International Development (USAID) created the Center for Private Business Reform, which provides aid for the restructuring of enterprises. Privatization through tenders and open auctions was expected to raise a total of US$22 million. Apart from individual projects, foreigners can buy small trading and service companies, as well as unfinished construction sites at open auctions.

ECONOMIC CHALLENGES

Moldova has faced many obstacles since 1991. According to government statistics, about 80% of the population live below the poverty level, and 10% of the rural population earns less than one-quarter of the poverty level. A majority of citizens cannot afford to buy fish, meat, milk, and other dairy products on a regular basis. Total estimated unemployment is 20%.

About 60% of the national economy is controlled by organized crime because of the lack of an adequate legal framework to fight economic crime. Problems arise because under the Soviet system, factories were all in one country, and processing or production took place in another. This worked well then, but now individual countries have enormous difficulties managing this separation. One-third of the 190,100 businesses registered in Moldova are not operating at present because of serious financial problems. Enterpreneurs are discouraged by the lack of state support, the many controls, and the bureaucratic procedures involving registration, issuance of licenses, and production certificates.

MOLDOVANS

MOLDOVA HAS A POPULATION DENSITY of 336 persons per square mile (130 persons per square km). This means Moldova has the highest population density among the republics of the former Soviet Union. It is also one of the most densely populated European countries. In comparison the United States has a density of only 60 per square mile (23 per square km).

POPULATION TRENDS

The population grew from 3 million to nearly 4.5 million in 30 years. This low growth rate is the result of a high mortality rate and a declining birth rate. Unlike most Western countries, the aging population is not growing fast because life expectancy is only 65 years of age. There are more males than females in the ages 0–14, but in all other groups, this trend is reversed. Sixty-five percent of Moldovans are employed.

Left: **Nine percent of the population are over the age of 65, and slightly more than 50% are female.**

Opposite: **Children constitute a large portion of the Moldovan population because the current annual birth rate is high, at 16.3 births per 1,000 people.**

WHERE PEOPLE LIVE

Moldova is one of the least urbanized republics of the former USSR. Forty-seven percent of the country's inhabitants live in cities, an increase from 13% in 1940. Moldovans reside in 21 cities and towns, 48 city-type settlements, and more than 1,600 villages. More than 60% of the urban population is concentrated in the major cities of Chisinau, Balti, Tiraspol, and Tighina with more than 33% in the capital of Chisinau. Sixty-eight percent of the rural population reside in towns and villages. With a high proportion of the population in rural areas, production per person is less than that in the former Soviet Union, but living standards are higher because food and consumer goods are easily available.

One of the residential districts in Chisinau.

THE ISSUE OF ETHNICITY

Moldova joins two different regions, Bessarabia and Transnistria, into one country. Bessarabia consists predominantly of ethnic Romanians and constitutes the western half of the country. Transnistria is Slavic, and its people are ethnic Ukrainians and Russians. Viewed as a whole, Moldova has a majority population of ethnic Romanians. Despite Soviet efforts to Slavicize them, most ethnic Romanians maintained their identity and looked to Romania as the source of their culture. When the Soviet Union crumbled, Moldova asserted its independence, although people were far from unanimous on the issue. The nationalists eventually succeeded. Moldova sought to distance itself from Russia. But the Transnistrians wanted no part of independent Moldova, its ethnic-Romanian nationalists, or reunification with Romania, where they would be a small minority instead of a powerful political force.

In the southwest the Gagauz have been campaigning for more autonomy in recent years. Their governor has said the main concerns are a poor knowledge of the official language because of the lack of teachers, handbooks, and reference materials and the attempt by some parliamentary factions to review the special juridical status the Gagauz now enjoy.

There is growing concern among Bulgarians living in the Taraclia district in the south of Moldova that their district might be abolished and incorporated into a larger district. This is viewed as an infringement of the rights and freedom of ethnic Bulgarians, following on the government's

The problem of ethnicity has dominated the political scene in Moldova since the late 1980s and has resulted in a civil war in which hundreds of people have been killed.

ETHNIC MIX

About 65% of the population are native Moldovans, while the other 35% consist of Ukrainians, Russians, and the Gagauz people. There are also a small number of Bulgarians and Jews. Other peoples include Belorussians, Poles, and Germans.

Ethnic Russian and Romanian children living harmoniously side by side.

decision in 1999 to close down the all-republican *Rodno Slovo* newspaper, published in the Bulgarian language. Deputies who are part of the Democratic and Prosperous Moldova Bloc pushed a legislative initiative to allow the Bulgarian population in the Taraclia district to have their own county within the boundaries of the Taraclia district. This move in favor of the Bulgarian population would lessen the possibility of tension in southern Moldova. The Communist Party also declared its full support for the Bulgarians' case.

Greek professor Alexis Heraclides has held seminars in the Moldovan parliament focusing on the situation of ethnic minorities in a democratic political system. He thinks the settlement of interethnic conflicts is about finding middle solutions that give important rights to the majority group, but also respect the rights of minority groups. His idea is not to reach an ideal settlement but avoid a dictatorship or separatism.

Children helping their father. Moldovans are by nature a hardworking people.

MOLDOVAN CHARACTER

Moldovans have managed to maintain strong family ties, tradition, a rich culture, and a love of beauty and the arts. Under Soviet rule, everything was done for the good of the community. This spirit is slowly dying out. In its place is the freedom to act according to one's interests. But this does not mean they have become self-centered. Moldovans are extremely friendly and kind . This is especially so in the villages, where the communal bond is close-knit. Moldovans love to socialize and make people feel comfortable. Friends will stop by each other's homes without prior notice because they know they will be welcome. People are also not aggressive or competitive by nature. Moldovans do not like to fight their own people. Any hostility or violence toward others is usually caused by the potent force of nationalism, where people hold different political opinions.

LOCAL CUSTOMS

Moldovan men always greet each other with a handshake. When a man sees a male acquaintance in a group and greets him with a handshake, it would be impolite not to shake the hands of all the males in the group as well. Unlike men, Moldovan women do not shake hands. In either a business or a social setting, a nod of the head is acceptable when greeting a woman.

In Moldova, shoes that are worn outdoors are removed when entering a home or apartment. Moldovans normally change into slippers indoors. A host would be extremely offended if guests were to wear their shoes in his home.

Below: **Visitors to the market are always greeted with smiles from the vendors.**

Opposite: **An elderly woman in traditional dress.**

TRADITIONAL DRESS

A distinctive feature of the Moldovan national dress is the embroidery present on both men's and women's clothes. The rich colors of red, black, and gold embroidery complement each other and contrast with a white background. A woman's blouse is loose fitting with three-quarter or full length sleeves, and worn with a white skirt. Over the skirt, a dark colored apron with woven geometric patterns is worn, tied at the waist with a sash. Regional differences are reflected in the colors and patterns of embroidery used. Cotton and silk, or wool for the winter, are the preferred fabrics. These clothes are traditionally spun and sewn by women. Colored scarves with a white border of lace are worn by women on their heads and tied under the back of the head. Strings of beads around the neck and long dangling pearl earrings complete the outfit.

The men's national dress is a long-sleeved white shirt, worn with narrow trousers that are secured at the waist with a sash or leather belt. An embroidered sleeveless vest is worn over the shirt. Headgear for men is a tall hat made of lambskin, felt, or even straw for the summer. Traditional footwear for both sexes is the moccasin, a type of soft leather slipper.

LIFESTYLE

SINCE 1991, LIFE FOR MOLDOVANS has changed, whether they live in urban centers or rural areas. Communist control, collective farming, social protection, and for some, the receipt of a regular paycheck, have been replaced by volatile market forces. Such adjustments can be very difficult for people who depended on the communist system all their lives.

Corruption and crime have increased significantly, and living standards have been reduced for the vast majority. There is now a growing gap between the rich and the poor in society. Despite these difficulties, Moldovans have retained their core values and traditions. Family, friends, and village communities remain close-knit, and parents have started to place more emphasis on their children's education. Most people hope that in the 21st century, with the worst behind them, they can enjoy the fruits of capitalism that they have been promised.

Left: **A young girl building a snowman.**

Opposite: **A student logs on to the Internet.**

LIFE EVENTS

To Moldovans, marriage is a major life event. Orthodox Christian couples typically marry in the Orthodox Church. After the church service, there is often a party in a restaurant with dancing and plenty to eat and drink. In the rural areas, any stranger who enters the village on the day of the marriage is invited to join in the festivities and is welcomed as part of the family. Local musicians play lively music, and tables are set up in a central communal area for the feast. Giving money rather than presents is a traditional custom at such weddings, and a plate is passed around to collect money for the couple.

Another happy occasion Moldovans celebrate is the birth of a child. If the infant's parents are Orthodox Christians, the child is christened in the church, and guests are invited to the parents' house for refreshments.

Funerals are solemn events, and the deceased is treated with utmost respect. At funerals the body is laid in an open casket, and mourners come to the house to pay their respects to the family. Food and drink, prepared by the family, are served to the mourners. Usually the burial is within three days of death. For Jews, the ceremony takes place within two days.

THE MOLDOVAN FAMILY

It is not unusual to find three-generation families living in the same house. Although this can be mainly attributed to the difficulty of finding housing, it is also a reflection of Moldovan family values. The family is very important to Moldovans, and the average urban family has two to three children. Rural familes may have more children.

From an early age, Moldovans are taught to respect and care for older people. Thus there are few nursing homes for the elderly and the disabled. Within a family, if there are older members, the rest would try their best to provide for them. Placing a family member in an institution is definitely a last resort.

Below: **A family posing for a photograph before their meal.**

Opposite: **A funeral procession in a village in northern Moldova.**

EDUCATION

Today 96% of the population aged 15 and above can read and write. At the beginning of the 20th century, illiteracy was common among Moldova's rural population. Under the Soviet system, education was made more available. However, this did not mean Moldovans spent many years in school. In 1990 the average number of years spent in school was only six, and only 30% of the population aged 15 and above had completed general secondary education. Under Moldova's new education system, there are significant improvements. Children have to attend 10 years of basic education, followed by either technical school or higher education. Moldovan students learn math and science at an early age.

Students are briefed before an examination.

School enrollment is about 1.52 million students. The teacher-student ratio is about 1:14 in the elementary system and 1:11 in secondary schools. The Ministry of Education has decided that all schools will reduce the school week from six to five days to lessen children's fatigue, save electrical costs by schools, and to be consistent with higher education institutions, offices, and industrial enterprises, which operate only five days a week.

There were only 10 students per 10,000 population enrolled in institutions of higher education in 1940. After the Soviet government eradicated illiteracy, this number increased to 120 per 10,000 population in 1992. In a year, Moldova spends approximately US$110 subsidizing each student in higher education. Moldova has about 73,000 students in its universities and has 38 institutions of higher education, of which 25 are private and 13 state-supported.

NEW EDUCATION PROGRAMS

The government has embarked on several programs to improve the quality of education in Moldova. One of them is called Project GLOBE. It is a student exchange program that involves participating schools in Moldova and Florida. English language classes are provided for Moldovans who plan to attend colleges and universities in Florida. The government hopes that when the students return to Moldova, they can apply their knowledge to the various sectors of the economy. For instance, graduates of the Moldovan Agricultural University study modern methods of agribusiness in the United States, so they can help their country privatize its large agricultural establishment. In turn, agriculture students from the University of Florida work and study on farms in Moldova to understand their methods of farming.

Through the Soros Foundation in Moldova, a media center has been opened since 1995 in the capital offering, among other things, seminars about how to operate a free and independent press. Moldovan journalists have had many opportunities to participate in education and training programs in Washington as part of the establishment of an independent media in Chisinau.

Healthy Moldovan children playing in a park.

HEALTH

Unlike the United States, healthcare in Moldova is paid for by the state and not by private insurance companies. In 1999 the Moldovan parliament passed a law called Guaranteed Minimum of Medical Assistance, which sets the amount of medical services that Moldovans can get for free. Under the new law, Moldovans do not have to pay for primary medical assistance by a family doctor, emergency aid before admission to a hospital, or medical care for an acute condition. Pregnant women and children will enjoy free medical care within the limits established by the government.

Although medical benefits for the people of Moldova are good, modern medical equipment and hospital facilities are in short supply. In 1990 there were approximately 129 hospital beds and 40 doctors per 10,000 inhabitants. In Moldova, a UN family planning program (UNFPA) has given priority to the area of reproductive health, in view of what they consider high abortion rates in the country and the limited availability of safe and reliable family planning methods. The objective of its assistance is to promote improved reproductive healthcare services and information, including family planning. The UNFPA provided funding for the First National Family Planning Conference and, together with the World Health Organization and the International Planned Parenthood Federation (IPPF), financed and facilitated two training workshops on reproductive health for the Family Planning District Coordinators of the Ministry of Health.

Tuberculosis infection is an ever-present problem for the health department. More than 2,000 Moldovans are infected with the disease annually. In 1998 Moldova had a influenza epidemic. Doctors have attributed this to general malnutrition, which has led to low resistance to infections. In just one week, the number of flu cases spread from only 85 to 1,800.

A dental clinic in Chisinau.

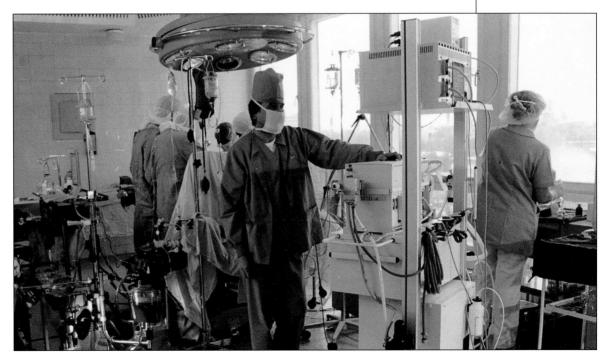

WOMEN'S ISSUES

Below: **Elena Burca, a deputy in parliament, talking to another deputy.**

Opposite: **More women are joining the workforce in an attempt to become financially independent.**

According to Ministry of Health statistics, more than 700 cases of breast cancer are reported every year in Moldova, and a total of 500 Moldovan women die from it annually. Breast cancer topped the list of malignant tumors in 1998 and overtook, for the first time, lung cancer. One in five patients suffering from breast cancer visited the doctor too late, when the chances of survival were reduced to the minimum. Concerns have been raised by women's groups that women's right to health is violated in Moldova. Every settlement in Moldova should have a center so that cancer can be detected early. However, adequate detection devices are lacking in Moldova. Even the main center at the Chisinau Oncological Institute

does not have a mammograph, a very basic piece of equipment that takes an x-ray photograph of the breasts. It facilitates early detection of breast cancer.

Since independence, there has been a substantial growth in domestic violence. According to statistics, one in four women in Moldova has been subject to physical or sexual violence at various times in her life. In 1997 and 1998, as many as 195 Moldovan women were killed in family quarrels. However, many women are no longer passive about such attacks. Figures in 1998 showed an increase in women who defended themselves, although some of them have resorted to unlawful means in retaliation. Twenty-eight percent of family murders were committed by women.

Continual poverty has led to a growing number of cases of child abuse. In 61% of abuse cases, it is the father who is responsible. Women's rights activists insist that the rights of children living in conflict zones should be better respected. They must, in particular, be provided with better conditions to study their mother tongue. Others, such as Russian human rights activists, have committed themselves to visit the Dniester region to observe the situation of children in eastern Moldova.

ORGANIZED CRIME

Over 15,000 crimes and offenses were reported in Moldova in 1998, of which 13,000 occurred in the capital. Throughout 1998, the number of people sentenced for murder, rape, and bodily injury increased significantly. There have been a growing number of hired murders, and more cases of robbery and terrorism have been reported. The European Union and the Council of Europe have launched a joint anticrime and anticorruption program in Moldova coded as Octopus-II. The program is designed to promote the principles of democracy and law, economic progress, and respect for human rights by imposing control on organized crime and corruption. In 1998 Moldovan judges punished 15,454 people. Some of them were sentenced to imprisonment, others ordered to do public work, and the rest were fined.

HOUSING

The most popular accomodation in the capital is a two-room apartment on the first or second floor of a five- to nine-floor building. Two-room apartments in 1999 cost between US$6,000 and US$10,000. The cost of housing dropped considerably in 1998. The reduction in prices was only for one-room and three-room apartments in the metropolitan sectors of Chisinau, which continue to be the most prestigious residential area. The fall in prices was partly due to the financial crisis in the same year and because supply exceeded demand three-fold in the real estate market.

Starting in March 1999, residents of Chisinau had hot water only twice a week, according to a decision by city hall. City officials said that the move was conditioned by the need to save money and reduce expenditures for these services.

In the countryside, people live in houses with some land to grow food for themselves. Rural living means living in small villlages, where the houses are clustered together.

Below: **The living quarters of poorer Moldovans.**

Opposite: **Graffiti or a work of art? Such "wall paintings" are commonly found in the cities.**

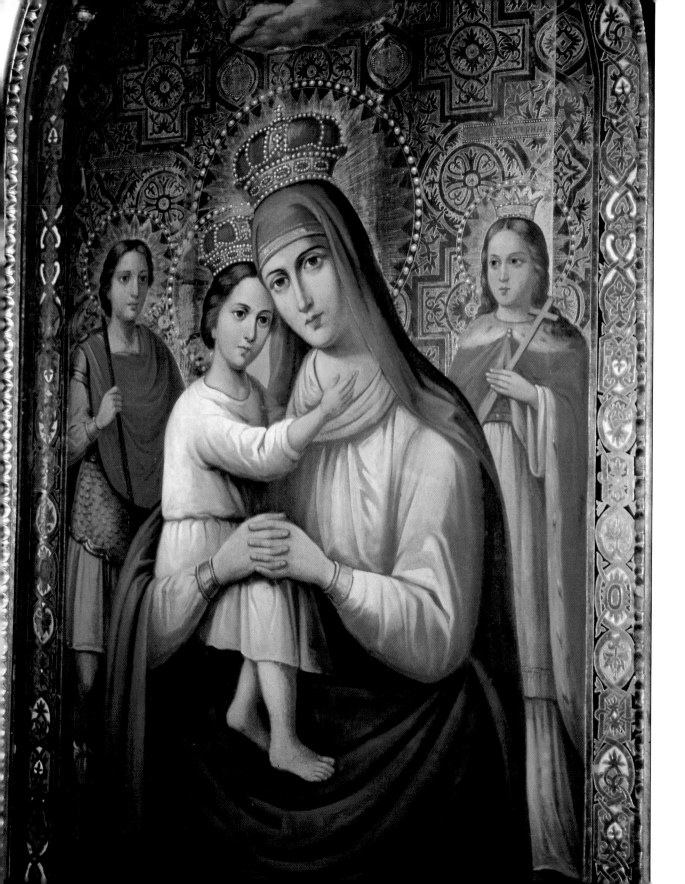

RELIGION

ABOUT 98.5% OF MOLDOVANS belong to the Eastern Orthodox Church, a branch of Christianity. The Moldovan Metropolitan Church is one branch of the Eastern Orthodox Church, which is a group of self-governing churches. It recognizes the honorary primacy of the Patriarch of Constantinople. Religious observances are now openly allowed, but such tolerance has not increased the numbers of churchgoers. On the contrary, like church attendance around the world, the number of churchgoers in Moldova has declined.

The other religious denominations are Uniate, Jewish, Armenian Apostolic, Seventh-Day Adventist, Baptist, and Pentecostal. There are more than 850 churches, 11 Christian Orthodox monasteries, two Armenian churches, and more than 60 churches of the Seventh-Day Adventists. There is one synagogue serving the Jewish community.

Left: **A newborn child is baptized at home.**

Opposite: **An icon of the Virgin Mary in a church in Chisinau.**

Overleaf (left): **Inside the walls of the ancient Virgin's Asuep Church of Causeni.**

Overleaf (right): **A church service in progress.**

EASTERN ORTHODOX CHURCH

The Eastern Orthodox Church is a Christian branch that separated from the Roman Catholic Church in the 11th century. The spilt between the two churches was related to the division of the Roman Empire into eastern and western halves—the eastern center being the city of Constantinople (now known as Istanbul) and the western center being Rome. Conflict over issues of doctrine led to an irreconcilable division, and the leader of the eastern part, the Patriarch of Constantinople, and the Pope of Rome, excommunicated each other. As a result of this divorce, the two branches went in quite distinct directions, largely due to the different cultures of the west and east.

For Eastern Christianity, mysticism is extremely important, and the idea of grace and the redeeming power of God's love is paramount. Eastern Christianity is found in Greece, Eastern Europe, the Middle East, and North Africa. According to many authorities, one of the reasons why the eastern liturgy has made a stronger impact on the Christian Church than its Western counterpart is that it has always been viewed as a total experience, appealing simultaneously to the emotional, intellectual, and aesthetic aspects of man. Western Christianity, on the other hand, portrays God as ultimately a judge. Followers of Western Christianity believe that one's actions on earth will influence whether one can go to heaven after death.

There have been recent negotiations between the heads of the Romanian and Russian Orthodox churches over the future of the church in Moldova. The Moldovan Metropolitan Church (MMC), represented by Bishop Vladimir, wants to be part of the Russian Orthodox Church. Meanwhile, an unofficial church, the Bessarabian Metropolitan Church (BMC), represented by Bishop Paduraru, wants to be part of the Romanian Orthodox Church.

Prime Minister Ion Sturza has been meeting with Bishop Vladimir of the MMC to discuss the issue of recognizing the BMC. He suggested that the two churches cooperate and live side by side in harmony. Eliminating clashes within the church is essential to the longevity of the Eastern Orthodox faith. Since 1992 the BMC has formally asked the Chisinau government to grant it legal status on several occasions, but they were refused each time. In June 1998 the Bessarabian Metropolitan Church sued the government in the European Court on human rights grounds, although they will withdraw their suit if the government deals with the problem directly.

Three priests preside over a festive occasion.

RELIGION UNDER SOVIET RULE

The Soviet government strictly limited religious activity and ordered the destruction of Orthodox churches in an attempt to destroy religion completely. Clergy were punished and sometimes imprisoned for leading services, but most orthodox believers continued to practice their religion in secret. By the beginning of World War II, the church structure was almost completely destroyed throughout the country. Many priests changed occupation.

The catastrophic course of combat in the beginning of World War II forced Stalin to mobilize all national resources for defense, including the Orthodox Church as the people's moral force. Without delay, churches were opened for services, and clergy were released from prisons. Between 1945 and 1959, the church hierachy was greatly expanded, although some members of the clergy were still occasionally arrested. This process can be described as a rapprochement between Church and State. The Church, however, always remained under state control. A new and widespread persecution of the Church was subsequently instituted under the leadership of Nikita Khrushchev and Leonid Brezhnev. Then, beginning in the late 1980s, under Mikhail Gorbachev, new political and social freedoms resulted in the lifting of the remaining restrictions. The collapse of the Soviet Union in 1991 led to religious freedom. Since then, churches have been restored and repaired in towns and villages. There is, however, a chronic lack of priests, and the recruitment of seminarians, or students training to be priests, is very low.

ORTHODOX VIEW

The concept that the church is most authentic when the congregation of the faithful is gathered together in worship is a basic expression of Eastern Christian experience. This explains the fundamental structure of the Orthodox Church, with the bishop functioning as a teacher and high priest in the liturgy. A richness of faith, spiritual significance, and variety of worship represents one of the most significant factors in this church's continuity and identity. It helps to account for the survival of Christianity during the many centuries of Muslim rule in the Middle East and the Balkans when the liturgy was the only source of religious knowledge or experience. The Orthodox Church has a firm conviction that the liturgy is the main vehicle and experience of true Christian beliefs. Consequently, reform of the liturgy is often considered equivalent to a reform of the faith itself. However inconvenient this conservatism may be, the Orthodox liturgy has preserved many essential Christian values transmitted directly from the experience of the early church.

Religion is an important part of the lives of Moldovans, including soldiers.

Overleaf: **Building a new church.**

CHURCH ARCHITECTURE

The highly decorated style of the Eastern Orthodox Church originated from the Byzantine era. This style of architecture, and icon painting, has since grown into an important Moldovan art. The physical splendor of the churches is emphasized, and a standard type of church—the cross was inscribed in a rectangle and the dome supported on piers—has become the accepted style for Orthodox churches. Over time, windows were narrowed, roofs became steeper, and flat-dome profiles assumed the rotund form, which eventually became the most notable feature of Orthodox Church architecture.

After Constantinople fell to the Turks in 1453, Russia launched a large-scale church building program. Church architecture began to lose the special features associated with the Byzantine heritage, becoming more national in character and increasingly illustrating the taste and thought of the people. The most important change in Russian church design in the 16th century was the introduction of the tiered tower and the tent-shaped roof, first developed in wood by Russia's carpenters. The basic types and structural forms of the Russian multicolumned and tented churches were fully developed in the 16th century.

IMPORTANCE OF ICONS

Icon is a Greek word meaning image. Icons are usually painted on a wooden base known as an icon board. The board consists of several parts bound together at the back by planks. The icon is placed on the face side of the board in a shallow rectangle or square groove (ark). Before painting begins, the board is covered with fabric, primed by a mixture of natural glue and chalk, then coated with an initial layer of dark reddish brown or greenish paint. Where needed, the color is made lighter with ochre or whiting. Radial lines were gold painted on the top of regular paint.

According to custom, an icon artist is expected to be a person of high morals and Christian ideals who prepares for his work by fasting and praying. The iconography is not a creation of the artist's imagination or whim, but follows a pattern and subject prescribed by church tradition. Sometimes icons had metal covers made for them to protect them from human handling in devotions, to enhance their beauty, or as memorials. The oklads often were made of silver or gilded silver, and the metal was cut out to reveal the painted faces, hands, and feet of the icon beneath. Some oklads were studded with precious gemstones, diamonds, and pearls.

In a church, small icons are set on portable, cloth-draped lecterns, and large ones are hung on the walls. Beeswax candles are burned nearby, and the icons are kissed, touched, and incense lit in front of them as acts of devotion. Icons are blessed with holy water and carried in processions both inside and outside the church. An icon of one of the 12 special liturgical feast days is often displayed on a lectern in the center of the church, according to the day of the feast. An icon of a special saint whose memory the church is honoring or an icon of the church's patron saint may also be placed in this central location. The faithful pray, make the sign of the cross, and display profound reverences, such as bowing, kneeling, kissing, and touching the forehead to the icon. Icons are venerated but never worshipped.

These acts of respect, handed down from ancient cultural traditions, still survive worldwide in the Orthodox Church. In Orthodox homes, icons are displayed in special places of honor. To the Orthodox Christian, an icon is a constant reminder of God's presence in his church, his home, and in his life. Icon painting flourishes in monasteries.

THE ROLE OF HYMNS

Throughout the centuries, the Orthodox liturgy has been richly embellished with cycles of hymns from a wide variety of sources. In the early centuries of the church, Christians sang in unison. The music used was never written down, but simply transmitted orally. It was not until the third century A.D. that a system of church melodies was put together. The use of instruments in Christian worship was discouraged by the early church fathers as they felt that the instruments distracted the mind from thoughts of God and turned them toward the self. The Book of Psalms played a central role in early Christian worship, and in the East, the method of chanting the psalms was well established by the end of the fourth century A.D.

Singing a hymm in celebration of a special occasion.

MONASTERIES

As in all of Eastern Europe, monasteries play a vital role in Moldova. Apart from their purely spiritual work, they are major centers of education. In particular, monasteries have recorded in their chronicles all the major historical events. They have also translated into Romanian various theological, historical, and literary works.

Capriana, 12 miles (20 km) northwest of Chisinau, is the site of the most celebrated 14th-century monastery. It lies amid the hills and is the most charming monastery in the countryside. Next to the old monastery, which has silver towers reaching to the high dome, is a new church with beautiful paintings that are slowly being restored. There is another famous monastery at Saharna, which is north of the capital and located on the Dniester River. This monastery is built underground. Thirty-one miles (50 km) north of Chisinau, near the Raut River, is the Cave Monastery. Built in the 15th century within a stony mound, this site had great tactical advantages and was used by Stephen the Great.

LANGUAGE

THE MOLDOVAN LANGUAGE is a symbol of national pride and cultural heritage. It was surpressed during Soviet rule, so now that the country is independent, everyone speaks Moldovan. Another language spoken in Moldova is Romanian. People who speak Romanian are able to understand Moldovan, and many consider the two to be essentially the same. Russian is the third major language, used for interethnic communication. For centuries, when Moldova was part of the Russian Empire, Russian was the official means of communication. Another language is that spoken by the Gagauz people. There are also local dialects heard in rural parts of the country.

Language is a divisive element in modern-day Moldova. Despite the respect minorities are shown, there is anger among ethnic Slavs who think that their language has been denigrated.

Left: **A schoolteacher reading to her students.**

Opposite: **A Moldovan woman reading the newspaper,** *The Communist,* **during an antigovernment rally.**

DEVELOPMENT OF MOLDOVAN

The Moldovan language can be traced back to Roman times. When the present-day Romanian and Moldavian territories were conquered by the Romans, the people living there had to adapt to the Roman language and culture. No script existed for "Romanian," the spoken language. The only written languages were Latin and Old Slavic, but at that time, only a few privileged people, such as clerics, scholars, and some noblemen, were able to understand Latin or Old Slavic.

The first known manuscript in the Romanian language appeared in 1420, although it was still written in Cyrillic characters. The actual development of the Romanian written script began in the 16th century. At that time, merchants and craftsmen needed a means of written communication to record their trade transactions without being obliged to learn Latin or Old Slavic, and so the Romanian written language was adopted. The written form of the Moldavian language developed later. Today, with its Latin script, the language is basically the same as Romanian. The only difference is in the phonetics and vocabulary. As Moldova once belonged to Romania, this similarity is easy to understand.

LANGUAGE POLICY FROM 1812 TO 1917

In 1812 Moldavia became part of the Russian Empire. The first Romanian school in Moldavia was established by G. Asuchi, who also edited the first Romanian newspaper. In official documents, Moldavian was declared the second national language. Russian was the first national language.

When Alexander I died in 1825 and Nicholas I came to the throne, the Moldavian people slowly lost their privileges, including their language rights. In 1828 their autonomous status was removed, Moldavians occupying posts in administration were replaced by Russians, the Russian legal and administrative systems were introduced, and Romanian schools were closed. From then until the Russian Revolution in 1917, Romanian could only be spoken in nonpublic areas. To pursue a career, knowledge of Russian was indispensable.

Above: **A road sign in Cyrillic and Moldovan.**

Opposite: **An ancient manuscript.**

Joseph Stalin in 1936.

LANGUAGE IN THE MOLDAVIAN SOCIALIST SOVIET REPUBLIC

From 1917 until Lenin's death in 1924, the country enjoyed a tolerant nationalistic language policy. All ethnic groups had equal rights, some even received privileges. Their native languages and cultures were promoted, linguists developed written forms of the spoken minority languages, and school lessons were conducted in native languages.

When Stalin came to power, he replaced non-Russians and nonconformist Russians in government, administration, and other public areas and replaced them with his Russian supporters. Russian became the local language, and learning it in school became compulsory. To improve one's social status, one had to learn Russian and adapt to Russian culture. The main aim of Stalin's policy was to deny that Moldavians and Romanians had been one people.

After Stalin's death in 1953, Khrushchev relaxed these policies, and it became possible again to take part in the cultural life of Romania. Romanian books were sold, and Romanian films were shown. There were even exchange programs organized between Moldavian and Romanian students, enterprises, and theaters.

In the mid-1960s, the situation worsened. An anti-Romanian campaign was started, and an emphasis was placed on the independence of Moldavia from Romania. Authors were criticized for Romanian language influences, and Romanian books and films were prohibited. Exchange programs were also no longer possible. By the 1970s, the situation improved slightly.

When Gorbachev became leader of the USSR in 1985, he implemented a policy of *glasnost* ("GLAS-nos") and *perestroika* ("perry-STROT-car"). These policies encouraged a public opposition movement consisting mainly of writers and linguists who criticized the language policies of the past. In 1988 the Mateevici Society was founded. Mateevici, an orthodox priest who died in 1917, had written a poem entitled *Limba Noastra* (Our Language). The main demand of this movement and other opposition groups was the promotion of an accurate interpretation of the Moldavian language and Moldovan history. They campaigned for increased visibility for Moldovan cultural features in public life, abolishment of mixed schools, and the establishment of separate schools for each nation. During final discussions in parliament, half a million people demonstrated for *Limba Noastra*.

Mikhail Gorbachev's policies in the late 1980s relaxed the tense situation and revived the literary circles in Moldova.

Finally, two laws were passed in August 1989 to correct the language policy and stress the independence of Moldovan and Russian culture. Moldavian, using the Cyrillic script, was declared the state language, to be used in political, economic, social, and cultural life. The intrinsic connection between the Romanian and Moldavian languages was officially recognized. Gagauzian became the second state language in areas with a high proportion of Gagauz people, and Russian was the language of communication among the different nationalities. After independence, Moldovans debated whether their language should be changed to the name "Moldovan." The president explained that "Moldovan" was used in the constitution for political reasons—to lessen the fears of those who opposed imminent reunification with Romania. The public response to the change in name was a resounding yes.

USE OF RUSSIAN BEFORE INDEPENDENCE

The rural population living in villages hardly had any contact with Russians, so there was no need for them to use Russian, which they learned at school. An exception was Moldovan men who had to do military service, since Russian was the only official language used by the Red Army, where people of different nationalities served together.

For the urban population, which had a high proportion of non-Moldovans, Russian was a common language. Until 1991, it was the language of everyday life. Speaking Russian in public was unavoidable for the urban population. Even today, most urban Moldovans are familiar with Russian.

THE MEDIA

Moldova's media is financed by public and private funding and has grown in the last few years. National and city governments subsidize a number of newspapers, but political parties and professional organizations, including trade unions, also publish newspapers. Although the number of private media outlets is growing, most of the independent media are still owned by politicians or have secured large sponsorships from these sources. These publications have the obligation to serve the interests of their sponsors.

The government does not restrict foreign publications. However, foreign publications do not have a wide circulation, since they are very expensive by local standards. Russian newspapers are available, and some of them publish a special Moldovan weekly supplement. There are more than a dozen daily newspapers and more than 500 weekly or monthly newspapers and magazines currently registered in Moldova.

There are several independent radio stations, including one that broadcasts religious programs. Nine AM radio stations and five FM stations operate in the main cities. Two independent television stations broadcast in the Chisinau area. The government owns and operates several major radio stations and a television channel. A number of regional centers, including Gagauzia, operate local television and radio stations.

Left: **A supplementary edition of the government newspaper, *Independent Moldova*. It is published in Russian and English.**

Opposite: **Learning English in an adult class. Educated Moldovans commonly speak French, English, Spanish, Italian, or German.**

ARTS

FROM A CULTURAL PERSPECTIVE, Moldova is a fascinating country. Theater, opera, dance, and music are Moldova's main performing arts. Visual arts are most evident in churches with their impressive frescoes. Traditional crafts, such as carving and embroidery, are also thriving.

CULTURAL TRADITIONS

Moldova's cultural traditions, influenced primarily by Romania, can be traced back to the period of Roman colonization in the second century A.D. Following the Roman withdrawal in A.D. 271, Moldova and Romania were next affected by the Byzantine Empire and later the Ottoman Turks. However, by the 14th century, a Moldovan identity began to emerge, while retaining close cultural links with Romanian groups. Eastern Moldovans were also influenced by Slavic culture from neighboring Ukraine.

Left: **A dance troupe in traditional dress.**

Opposite: **A Moldovan sits proudly on the porch of his elaborately decorated house.**

FOLK CULTURE

Soviet rule resulted in many ethnic Romanian intellectuals leaving the country to avoid being killed or deported both during and after World War II. With their departure, Romanian cultural influences diminished. Soviet authorities developed cultural and scientific centers and institutions that were filled with Russians and with other non-Romanian ethnic groups. The rural, ethnic Romanian population was allowed to express itself only in folklore and folk art. Although folk arts flourished, any that showed Romanian cultural influence were destroyed by the Soviets. For instance, the Romanian moccasin was replaced by Russian boots. Since independence, the moccasin has been brought back.

Folk traditions, including ceramics and weaving, continue to be practiced in rural areas. Handmade wool rugs, glass, intricate woodcarvings, earth-colored and black-colored pottery pieces, native dress, tablecloths, wooden boxes, and dolls are some examples of the traditional crafts still produced today in Moldova.

PAINTING

Moldova's artists have never enjoyed a worldwide reputation, neither in the past nor in contemporary times. However, a number have achieved some success outside of Moldova.

CHURCH FRESCOES

A fresco is a painting done with water-based pigments on a wall or ceiling while the plaster is still wet. Frescoes adorn churches in Moldova and are examples of art that portray life in the Middle Ages. Some of the monastries also have painted exterior walls that date from the 15th and 16th centuries. Most of them depict saints and the possible punishments or rewards awaiting the faithful in the next life.

FAMOUS MOLDOVAN PAINTERS

Valentin Koryakin was born in 1933 in Siberi. He graduated from the Belorussian Theater Art Institute in 1966. A member of the Union of Moldovan Artists since 1969, his work has been exhibited at many prestigious international exhibitions in countries such as France, Germany, Switzerland, Russia, and Belarus. Some of his more famous pieces are in the Chisinau museum and other museums throughout Eastern Europe. They are also kept by private collectors in the United States, Israel, Japan, and Canada.

Vitaliy Tiseev was born in 1935 in Moldova and studied at the Ilia Repin Art College in Chisinau from 1959 to 1964. In his professional career, he has produced a series of paintings devoted to Moldova. His work is sold to art galleries, museums, and private collectors throughout the art world in Europe, the United States, Canada, Israel, and India. His works have also been published in many magazines and books. His daughter Tatiana and son Sergey are also painters.

Other important artists are Dmitriy Kharin, Anna Ravliuk, and Mihai Brunea, who is the vice-president of the Artists Union of the Republic of Moldova.

A traditional music group performing in a park.

MUSIC

The S. Rakhmaninov and Ciprian Porumbescu music schools are prestigous places to study and have contributed greatly to Moldova's musical traditions. Composer Evgeny Doga, a Moldovan, is well known in Eastern Europe. The Moldovan Academy Ensemble, under the direction of Rector Constantin Rusnac, has performed in European and international competitions and has won many awards for its chamber concerts and renditions of native folk music. The Academy of Music in Chisinau is one of Eastern Europe's oldest and most distinguished conservatories. Graduates play in the finest symphonies and chamber orchestras in Europe and the United States. A 10-person music ensemble from the academy toured five Florida cities during the winter of 1994, playing in concerts of classical and Moldavian folk music.

The National Philharmonic Society travels widely to other European countries to perform and is held in high regard everywhere it is heard. Their interpretation of Ludwig van Beethoven's Symphony No. 9, often performed with the Doina Choir, is very popular among classical music enthusiasts. The orchestra has repeatedly performed this magnificent piece at many concerts, and in 1999 it celebrated the 175th anniversary of its first public performance. Another performance that delights Moldovans is Brahms' Symphony No. 1. When playing at home, the Moldovan Philharmonic frequently invites Romanian musicians to join them, providing an opportunity for promising young musicians to conduct their symphonic orchestra.

A concert in the Organ Hall in Chisinau.

MONUMENTS AND STATUES

Along the main boulevard in Chisinau is a statue of Kotovski. In the 1920s Kotovski attacked Romania in a series of raids. Today, some Moldovans see him as a Moldovan Robin Hood, while others consider him a bandit.

Stalinist blocks and neoclassical buildings can be found along the capital's main boulevard. On one corner of the Piata Nationala Square stands the statue of the legendary Stefan cel Mare, or Stephen the Great, the Romanian prince and national hero. This statue, which was made in 1928, had to be moved several times during World War II to save it from falling into enemy hands. Under Soviet rule, it was transported to a more obscure place in the park. After independence, the statue was brought back to its initial location. In the 1940s the Soviets replaced it with a statue of Lenin. In front of the History Museum is a statue of a she-wolf, feeding the two founders of Rome, Romulus and Remus. This serves as a reminder of the country's Latin ancestors.

The monument of the she-wolf and the legendary founders of Rome.

A FAMOUS MONUMENT

In the spring of 1999, more than 1,000 people attended the unveiling ceremony of a monument to Moldova's most beloved ballad singers, Ion and Doina Aldea-Teodorovici, who were killed in a car accident in neighboring Romania in October 1992. The couple were known as promoters of the national cause. Ion Aldea-Teodorovici, composer and singer, was born in 1954 in southern Moldova. Doina, his wife and band partner, was born in 1958 in Chisinau. The peak of their careers came in 1989–1992, when Moldova gained its independence.

The bronze monument stands near the national university. A local sculptor, Iurie Canasin, an architect, Nico Zaporojan, and a businessman, Anatol Josanu who financed the project, worked together in partnership. The ceremony was attended by President Petru Lucinschi, various officials, the couple's parents and son, artists, composers, singers, business people, and students, all of whom laid flowers at the memorial.

THEATER

Moldova has 12 professional theaters. Chisinau offers the most choices for theatergoers, but there are many small theaters outside of the capital. Members of ethnic minorities manage a number of folklore groups and amateur theaters throughout the country.

At the major theaters, performances are in Moldovan, except at the Chekhov Drama Theater in Chisinau and the Russian Drama Theater in Tiraspol, both of which perform solely in Russian. The Licurici Republic Puppet Theater in Chisinau performs in both Romanian and Russian.

The National Palace Theater with its stylish Corinthian columns and orange facade has shows throughout the year, although the month of

A Russian drama theater group after performing a folk tale.

March marks the start of traditional music and dance. Apart from the National Palace Theater, the Opera and Ballet Theater is a great place to hear piano and organ concerts and musical performances by local and visiting guests.

There are also a variety of other theaters— Satiricus, Ginta Latina, Luceafarul, Eugen Ionescu, and Mateevici. Theater tours to the United States by the highly-regarded Ionescu Theater performing classical plays are common. The Chisinau marionette theater opens its theatrical season in February.

LITERARY TRADITIONS

The first Moldovan books were religious texts that appeared in the mid-17th century. The oldest, original Moldavian manuscript still exists. It was written in 1429. Elaborately authored and illustrated books and manuscripts were produced in monasteries from the 13th and 14th centuries. They were extremely expensive to produce at that time. When the printing press became common, making books became easier and cheaper. Today, there are book exhibitions to encourage literary exchange and to introduce the younger generation to well-known writers of the past. One such exhibition is the 10-day Mihai Eminescu Memorial Days.

MIHAI EMINESCU

Mihai Eminescu represents the blinding pinnacle of Romanian and Moldovan literature and poetry. A national poet in both countries, his poems evoke beautifully the nature and soul of the people. In his work, all the national characteristics come to life. His poems combine his thoughts, sensibility, and creativity.

Eminescu was born in 1850. By 1866 he had published his first poem, signed with his real name, M. Eminoviciu. Joining the National Theater, he met Veronica Micle, who became the great love of his life. He held a number of jobs but continued to write and publish his poetry until he fell ill in 1884. He died in 1889. Here is one of his poems:

WHAT IS LOVE ...

What is love? A lifetime spent
Of days that pain does fill,
That thousand tears can't content,
But asks for tears still.
With but a little glance coquet
Your soul it knows to tie,
That of its spell you can't forget
Until the day you die.
Upon your threshold does it stand,
In every nook conspire,
That you may whisper hand in hand
Your tale of heart's aspire.
Till fades the very earth and sky,
Your heart completely broken,
And all the world hangs on a sigh,
A word but partly spoken.
It follows you for weeks and weeks
And in your soul assembles
The memory of blushing cheeks
And eyelash fair that trembles.
It comes to you a sudden ray
As though of starlight's spending,
How many and many a time each day
And every night unending.

For of your life has fate decreed
That pain shall it enfold,
As does the clinging waterweed
About a swimmer hold.

(English version by Corneliu M. Popescu)

Opposite: **A girl surrounded by books. Children are encouraged to read from an early age.**

LEISURE

LEISURE PURSUITS IN MOLDOVA are varied. In rural areas, activities tend to center around village life. On the weekend, the more well-to-do urban Moldovans attend the theater and concerts. For young people working in the cities, weekends provide an opportunity for them to return to their parents' home for a visit.

RELAXING AT HOME

Moldovans love to invite friends and family home for a meal. Friends often stop by a person's house without prior notice, and the reception is always friendly. Sometimes, even strangers are welcomed into Moldovan homes. When friends gather, they like to play boardgames as a way of passing time. Boardgames also have the advantage of involving the entire family. Among the different games, chess is the most popular.

On weekdays, after work, most people spend their time watching television or a movie video. In the past there were few program choices, and much of it was for propaganda purposes. Now people have more choices on the main television channels. Listening to the radio is also a popular pastime. Despite an increase in television viewers, this form of entertainment has managed to keep its audience.

With more than 500 daily, weekly, and monthly newspapers and magazines in Moldova, reading newpapers and magazines is a common activity. As a result, the average person is very well informed about local politics and world events.

Opposite: **Circus performers saluting the audience after their performance.**

CIRCUS TIME

Chisinau also has a wonderful circus run by the government. Performances are held in a giant circular-domed building. The circus has 158 staff. Performing animals, acrobats, and clowns entertain the crowd. Traveling circuses, such as those from China and Russia, are also hosted here.

В главной роли: Эмилио Дизи
В ролях: Морио Касси, Вируго Карамбула.
·Аргентина·
PLAJA
...BUNA
...щедший пляж

Un film de mare succes
avindu-l ca protagonist
pe celebrul
S. Stallone
RAMBO - FIRST BLOOD
...MBO
...О - ПЕРВАЯ ...
...Д.П.Косм...
...Сталлоне

Автор сценария: В.Москаленко
Режиссер: М. Туманишвили
При участии: Ю. Коротнова, Ю.Разыкова.
CIINELE
L...P
·Волко...

CEL M...

Moviegoers deciding which film to watch.

CONCERTS AND THEATER

Attending music concerts, whether rock, classical, or folk, or watching dramatic plays are popular forms of entertainment for Moldovans. The numerous musical events are a legacy from the Soviets, who frequently had musicians and singers perform in the various factories as a means of keeping the workers happy and satisfied. With enormous government subsidies for the arts, going to the theater was an affordable outing in the Soviet days. Unfortunately, such financial support has now been drastically reduced, and market forces are slowly being introduced. The result is a significant decline in concert attendance because few people can afford the high ticket prices.

Movie-going used to be a favorite activity among younger Moldovans, since there are many movies in Moldovan and Russian, as well as Hollywood films depicting their favorite movie stars. However, as home videos become cheaper and more accessible to the general public, the cinema is slowly losing its audience.

OUTDOOR PURSUITS

Moldova's climate is ideal for outdoor activities as the summers are never too hot, rainfall is sparse, and the winters are short compared to other countries in this part of the world. Geographically, the terrain is limited with no sandy beaches to play ball or mountains to climb. Nevertheless, walking in the parks in towns and cities can be very relaxing, and exploring the countryside, coupled with a family picnic by a lake, is a pleasant way to spend the weekend.

Hiking in the heavily forested Codri Hills is an experience that Moldovans especially enjoy in the spring and fall. The advantage of a small country is that such rural areas are easily accessible to city dwellers.

A family hiking in the Codri Hills. As the country's nature reserve is located in the Codri Hills, hiking has become a very pleasurable activity, with lots to see.

RURAL ACTIVITIES

Under the Soviet system, free time for young people was strictly monitored, especially in the cities. It was important for them to be doing something productive all the time, such as playing the piano, going to music school, or participating in sports like wrestling or weightlifting. Leisure in the rural parts of the country, however, was more relaxed, and children could do what they like. Leisure activities have not changed much since independence and are still conducted along traditional gender lines. Men occupy their free time with wood-carving and perhaps some furniture-making. They may gather in a group while engaging in such activities, so there is a fair amount of idle chatter and gossip.

Women spend their free time doing embroidery, or making dresses and quilts, as being idle is frowned on. These activities are carried out in a group setting, so talking and sharing a joke are part of the enjoyment. Passing on traditional stories that have a moral or a message about life by word of mouth to younger members of the community is prevalent throughout the countryside. Children love these stories, and it helps to connect them with the history and traditions of their motherland.

SPORTS

Football, or soccer, is unsurpassed as the main sport in Moldova from both the player's and spectator's perspective. It is popular with young and old alike, and is actively promoted in school. In the evenings, a group of young men can typically be found playing a friendly game or simply kicking a ball around. Tennis is also popular, and the National Tennis School has produced some excellent players who have done well in national and international competitions.

Palaces of Culture are popular sports recreation centers for children. Many sports and activities are available to meet different interests, such as soccer, tennis, swimming, judo, karate, and—for the more intellectual—chess. In Soviet times, these social centers or clubs were owned by the government, but they are now privately owned and are much more expensive, so the number of people using the facilities has dropped.

Two current soccer players with records for goals and appearances are Igor Oprea and Vasile Cosolev.

Left: **Moldova playing against Finland in a soccer match.**

Opposite: **Enjoying a game of basketball after school.**

FESTIVALS

MOLDOVA HAS RELIGIOUS HOLIDAYS, pagan festivals, and celebrations for national events. Since many people still live in the rural countryside, the celebration of traditional festivals continues to survive. There are also many established music and dance festivals.

NEW YEAR'S DAY

Unlike Americans, Moldovans do not hold large-scale, public New Year's Eve parties to usher in the new year. The most common celebration is having friends and family sit down together for a special meal and champagne. After the meal everyone gathers around the television to watch the countdown to midnight. On New Year's Day children go door-to-door with songs and poems. It is customary to give them small amounts of money or candy.

Left: **Friends and family sit down for a New Year's Eve dinner. This is a good time to extend greetings of good wishes and good health.**

Opposite: **Children offer food to the crowd during the feast of Chisinau.**

EASTER

Easter was not an officially celebrated holiday when Moldova was part of the Soviet Union. Nevertheless it has always been an important religious event for Moldovans, who are pious people. Easter starts with Palm Sunday, which is the day Jesus entered Jerusalem riding on a donkey.

On this day, palm leaves are hung in churches and homes. The days after Palm Sunday are Lent, a period of 40 days that includes fasting or some other kind of sacrifice, which represents the time Jesus spent preparing for his own death. Good Friday marks the day of the cruxifixion, and Easter Sunday is a day of joy for Christians because Jesus rose from the dead and ascended to heaven.

Easter is an important holiday in Moldova, with celebrations lasting for a week. In the Orthodox Church, Easter is held about three to four weeks later than Easter celebrations in the West. On the Orthodox clerical calendar, Easter usually falls during the month of April. On Easter Monday, people visit and pray at the graves of loved ones. This ritual symbolizes the hope that their family members have gone to heaven just as Jesus did.

CHRISTMAS

When Moldova was part of the Soviet Union, Christmas was not openly celebrated or officially acknowledged. However, it provided Moldovans with an opportunity to make merry and feast, and a huge family celebration was usually held.

The festive season begins with St. Nicholas' Day on December 6, when preparations for the big event officially start. Any special food that needs to be prepared ahead for Christmas would be made at this time. Shopping for new clothes or presents, or buying materials to make new clothes is a major activity for Moldovans.

Between December 6 and the end of the month, there are traditional practices that represent the end of one year and the approach of a new one. One such custom in the countryside is the pulling of a plow through a residential area to symbolize the cutting of a furrow. This is believed to bring prosperity to the people living there. The plow is decorated with leaves, which represent fertility and growth.

Above: **Santa Clauses celebrating Christmas. This happy occasion is not complete without his presence.**

Opposite: **An elderly man visits the grave of a loved one during Easter.**

Christmas Eve and Christmas Day, which fall on December 24 and 25 respectively, are spent with family members. There is generally a lot of eating and drinking, and everyone has a wonderful time. It is customary for families to gather together for a festive meal. Going to church on this day is an important activity. It reminds people that the true meaning of Christmas is the birth of Christ.

FESTIVAL OF THE TRANSFIGURATION

This festival, which takes place in August, commemorates the day when Jesus Christ took three of his disciples, Peter, James, and John, up to a mountain where Moses and Elijah appeared. According to the gospel, Jesus was transfigured on this day—his face and clothes became white and shining.

In the Orthodox Church, the Festival of the Transfiguration has always been a major festival. It celebrates the revelation of the eternal glory of the Second Person of the Trinity, which was normally veiled during Christ's life on earth. It is not known when the festival was first celebrated, but it was observed in Jerusalem as early as the seventh century and in most parts of the Byzantine Empire by the ninth century.

SECULAR HOLIDAYS

On March 8, in honor of Women's Day, gifts of candy and flowers are given to women. The intent of the holiday is similiar to St. Valentine's Day, but romance is not necessarily present. Gifts are meant to be small and inexpensive and represent friendship and best wishes for the future.

May 1 was a major event before independence. There were military marches and parades in honor of the workers, and local officials made public speeches. It is still a holiday today, although the military marches have all but disappeared. Moldovans now take the opportunity to go to the countryside, have a picnic, and enjoy the lovely spring weather after a long, dreary winter.

Below: **Enjoying the outdoors with a picnic on May 1.**

Opposite: **Celebrating the Festival of the Transfiguration in church.**

TRADITIONAL FESTIVALS

The month of March normally marks the start of a traditional music and dance festival. This is spring time, and the festival marks the rebirth of nature after winter. During this lively festival, classical and folk music predominate. A legacy of communist rule was that every town had an orchestra and conductor. Folk music is heard throughout the spring and summer.

The international music festival is attended by Russian, German, and American artistes. The festival usually opens with a performance focusing on traditional spring customs. Additional concerts are hosted by the Organ Hall, the National Opera, and the National Philharmonic. The festival is organized by the Ministry of Culture with the financial support of the Moldovan cabinet.

The music and dance festival, celebrated when spring arrives, reminds Moldovans of a time when people were more in touch with nature and the natural order of life.

This festival is the time when the traditional custom of honoring women is observed throughout the country. The music festival includes an exclusive performance for women, scheduled on Women's Day. It is attended by Moldovan musicians and fashion groups.

MAIN JEWISH HOLIDAYS

There are a small number of Jews in Moldova, and they celebrate a few Jewish festivals. The Jewish holiday of Rosh Hashanah, usually celebrated in September, is widely known and celebrated as the New Year's Day of the Jewish calendar. Rosh Hashanah has a fourfold meaning—the Jewish New Year, the Day of Judgement, the Day of Remembrance, and the Day of Shofar Blowing. It is the Day of Judgement as Jews across the world examine their past deeds and ask for forgiveness for their sins. On the Day of Shofar Blowing, the Shofar, or ram's horn, is blown in the temple to herald the beginning of the 10-day period. On the Day of Remembrance, the Jews review the history of their people and pray for Israel. New Year's Day is celebrated with greeting cards, prayers, and festive foods. Yom Kippur, the Day of Atonement, is the most sacred of the Jewish holidays. Those who have repented for their sins are granted a good New Year.

Passover commemorates the time when the Israelites were enslaved by the Egyptians, around 3,000 years ago. According to the Book of Exodus, Moses, a simple Jewish shepherd, was instructed by God to warn the Pharaoh that God would severely punish Egypt if the Israelites were not freed. The Pharaoh ignored Moses' request. In response, God unleashed a series of 10 terrible plagues on the people of Egypt.

When the Pharaoh agreed to free the Israelites, his army chased them through the desert toward the Red Sea. The waves of the Red Sea parted, and the Israelites were able to cross to the other side. As soon as they all reached the other side, the waves came together again, trapping the Pharaoh's army as the waves closed on them.

FOOD

THE SOVIET SYSTEM OF COLLECTIVE FARMING has worked well in Moldova as it is primarily an agricultural country. There is no shortage of food. Meat, vegetables, dairy products, and fruit are obtainable all year around. Although the cost of living rose dramatically in the 1990s, most people could still afford basic food necessities.

A SOCIAL OCCASION

Eating in Moldova is much more than simply consuming food to stay alive. Enjoyment of food in the company of others is paramount. The sharing of food together as a group is an established and highly valued Moldovan custom. It is customary when visiting friends or family to have something to eat and drink. The host will be disappointed if the offer is refused. Casual dining is by far the norm.

Left: **Two friends engaged in a game of arm-wrestling after dinner.**

Opposite: **Supermarkets like this one are common in the major cities, especially Chisinau.**

MEAL PATTERNS

Typically the main meal of the day is at midday, even for those who are working. People tend to get up early and have a light breakfast, usually some bread or pastry, and then have a hearty lunch. There are lots of restaurants and cafés offering snacks inside office buildings for employees.

DAILY MEALS

An everyday meal begins with a choice of many different soups, followed by a main dish of either fried meat or baked chicken, or salted or pickled fish. Smoked meats are sometimes eaten with fried potatoes and boiled vegetables as accompaniment. Rice, stuffed cabbage, cucumbers, and tomato salad are quite popular among Moldovans. A cheese is often served as a conclusion to the meal. Baked food and casseroles are the favorite foods of most people, appearing often on the daily menu of local restaurants.

Bread is an important and relatively cheap staple that is eaten at most meals. Its production has always been subsidized by the government, so as to keep it affordable to the general public. Bread lines were not uncommon under communist rule.

THE MOLDOVAN KITCHEN

The inside of a Moldovan kitchen is very similiar to one in the United States, although there are not so many labor-saving devices. A coffee maker would be an unusual item to find in the kitchen as coffee is made expresso style. An electric kettle, on the other hand, is indispensible. Preparing a meal, predominantly a woman's job, is time consuming as dishes are prepared from scratch. Popping a precooked meal into the microwave oven at the end of a hard day's work would be a luxury for the average Moldovan woman.

Except for salt, bay leaves, onions, and garlic, relatively few seasonings or spices are used in the flavoring of food. A lot of animal fat, oil, butter, and mayonnaise are used, and food is usually fried. Meat constitutes a major part of the diet.

Above: **A typical Moldovan kitchen.**

Opposite: **A family enjoying their lunch. On the table is homemade bread, cheese, and pork.**

Picking peaches in an orchard. The peach is a popular fruit among Moldovans because it is juicy and sweet.

FRESH PRODUCE

The rich soil and abundant rainfall in Moldova has resulted in ideal conditions for growing many kinds of vegetables and fruit. Cabbages, potatoes, carrots, beets, and turnips are the common crops. In addition, there are tomatoes, peppers, zucchini, cucumbers, eggplants, and lettuce.

There are plenty of orchards in the valleys of the Codri Hills. The orchards produce apples, plums, peaches, apricots, and walnuts. In autumn the bark of the apple trees is wrapped with thick strips of cloth to protect the bark from being burned by the sun or eaten by animals. A greater variety of fruit, such as strawberries, raspberries, and grapes, is available in the summer.

Farmers raise pigs, goats, poultry, and sheep throughout the country. Pigs in particular are plentiful, as pork is a popular dish.

TRADITIONAL CUISINE

Mamaliga ("mah-me-LI-ga"), a cornmeal mush, is the national dish. Traditionally, *mamaliga* was made in a cast iron kettle over an open fire and given to farm workers as a cheap, yet filling meal. People sometimes eat it cold for breakfast. Moldovans enjoy *mamaliga* when it is served with *ghiveci* ("GHEE-vetch"), a vegetable dish, and mushrooms sauteed in a wine and herb sauce.

Mititei ("me-tee-TAY") are grilled meatballs made from pork mixed with beef or lamb. Usually cooked outdoors over charcoal, they are eaten as a snack or as an appetizer and are sold by street vendors in the cities. *Mititei* is usually consumed with a glass of beer or wine.

Sarmale ("sar-MALL-eh") consists of cabbage or grape leaves stuffed with rice, meat, and herbs. The filling can be cooked in tomato or lemon sauce. The finished product is often served with cream.

Borsch ("BOR-sher"), a rich-tasting beet and vegetable soup, is actually an Ukrainian national dish and a great favorite in Moldova. Yogurt is used to make its texture silky. *Ciorba* ("CHOR-ba") is a sour-tasting soup that is traditionally made from the fermented juice of wheat bran. Lemon juice is now used as a substitute to make the sour base.

Brinza ("BRIHN-zah"), a cheese made from sheep's milk, is cured in brine. It is creamy, rich, and salty, ranging from soft and spreadable to semidry and crumbly.

Common desserts are *placinte* ("pla-CHIN-te"), which are similiar to turnovers, and *baklava* ("ba-KLA-va"), a Turkish pastry with crushed pistachios or almonds glazed with thick syrup. The result is an extremely rich and sweet dessert.

Preparations for a meat dish called *costita* ("cos-TEE-tah").

TRADITIONAL DRINKS

Homemade alcohol, although illegal, is still prepared in parts of the country. It is extremely potent and certainly an acquired taste. Wine and beer are more popular and are legally available. Moldova is well known for its fine cognac and brandy.

Tea is widely consumed, but Turkish-style coffee is far more common. It is usually drunk black, served in small cups and is very strong and sweet. Water or sometimes milk accompanies daily meals. Lemonade is a popular choice to quench one's thirst.

WINE

Moldova is one of the most interesting wine areas in Europe with great potential for future growth. Historically wine has been made in this area since the seventh century B.C. Moldova lies on the same latitude as the greatest wine-producing country, France, although its wine production is much smaller.

Moldovan wines were used by the Soviet Union as a source of cheap and readily available alcohol. Today the focus is on improving the quality of the wine rather than producing it in mass quantity. The very best wine is pressed and kept in oak barrels for many years.

GHIVECI

2 potatoes, quartered and sliced
$^1/_2$ head cauliflower, separated into flowerets
$^1/_2$ eggplant, cubed
2 carrots, sliced
1 small green or yellow summer squash, sliced
2 medium-sized onions, quartered and sliced
$^1/_2$ cup green peas
$^1/_2$ cup green beans, cut
1 green or red bell pepper, seeded and cut in chunks
2 ribs celery, sliced
17 oz (478 g) can plum tomatoes with liquid
$1^1/_2$ cups vegetable bouillon
$^1/_2$ cup pure olive oil
2 cloves garlic, chopped
salt and ground black pepper to taste
$^1/_2$ cup fresh dill and parsley, chopped

Preheat oven to 350°F (178°C). Place the potatoes, cauliflower, eggplant, carrots, summer squash, onions, green peas, green beans, pepper, and celery in a three- or four-quart ungreased casserole dish. Pour the tomatoes on top. Mix the bouillon, olive oil, and garlic, then pour this mixture over the vegetables. Season with salt and pepper to taste, and stir all ingredients once or twice.

Sprinkle the dill and parsley on top. Cover the casserole dish and bake at least one hour, or until the vegetables are of desired tenderness. Allow to cool a bit before serving over rice or *mamaliga*.

RESTAURANTS

Most local restaurants in the main cities serve a basic meal that costs much less than a meal in a Western restaurant. Chisinau has some restaurants with beautiful interiors. Dinner at these formal dining places are more expensive. Some of them have music performances during dinner hours.

There are many different ethnic restaurants in Chisinau offering Indian, Mexican, Korean, Chinese, Jewish, and Italian cuisine. Fast food restaurants sell hamburgers, fries, and pizza. An internationally known fast food chain has recently opened in Chisinau. Outside of lunch during the working day, eating out is uncommon for the average Moldovan.

Opposite: **An old wine-extracting press in the Museum of Viniculture and Viticulture in Chisinau. Queen Victoria of England was known to have a liking for Moldovan wine.**

MOLDOVA

A   B   C   D

1

2

3

4

5

Capital city
Major town
▲ Mountain peak

Feet   Meters
1,650   500
660   200
0   0

Dniester

● Edinti

● Soroca

Raut

● Drochia

● Floresti

Rezina ● ● Rabnita

Balti ●   Saharna ●

UKRAINE

Prut

Tipova ●

Falesti ●

Bessarabian

Codri

Orhei ●

Transnistria

Mount Balanesti
(1,407 ft / 429 m)

▲   ● Calarasi

Dubasari ●

Dniester

● Ungheni

Capriana ●

Hills

Ikel

● CHISINAU

ROMANIA

Bac

Upland

● Hancesti

Tighina ● ● Tiraspol

Botna

● Jura

● Causeni

Cogalnic

Plain

● Leova

Bugeac

● Comrat

Ialpug

● Ciadar-Lunga

Gagauzia

Prut

N

Black

Sea

0   25   50 Miles
0   25   50   75 Kilometers

Bac River, C3
Balanesti, Mount, B3
Balti, B2
Bessarabian Upland,
  B2–C4
Black Sea, D5
Botna River, C3
Bugeac Plain, C4–D4

Calarasi, B3
Capriana, C3
Causeni, C3
Chisinau, C3
Ciadar-Lunga, C4
Codri Hills, B2–C3
Cogalnic River, C3–C4
Comrat, C4

Dniester River, B1–C3
Drochia, B2

Dubasari, C3

Edinti, B1

Falesti, B2
Floresti, B2

Gagauzia, B4–C4

Hancesti, C3

Ialpug River, C4
Ikel River, C3

Jura, C3

Leova, B4

Orhei, C2

Prut River, B2–B5

Rabnita, C2
Rezina, C2
Romania, A3–B3
Raut River, B1–B2

Saharna, C2
Soroca, B1

Tighina, C3
Tipova, C2
Tiraspol, D3
Transnistria, C2–C3

Ukraine, C2–D2
Ungheni, B3

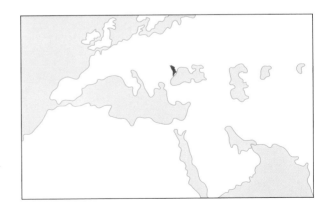

QUICK NOTES

OFFICIAL NAME
Republic of Moldova

NATIONAL FLAG
Blue, yellow, and red vertical bands; emblem in the center is a Roman eagle.

LOCATION
Eastern Europe, northeast of Romania

TOTAL AREA
13,047 square miles (33,800 square km)

CAPITAL
Chisinau

MAJOR CITIES
Tiraspol, Balti, Tighina

MAJOR RIVERS
Dniester, Raut, Ialpug, Cogalnic

CLIMATE
Moderate winters, warm summers

HIGHEST POINT
Mount Balanesti (1,407 ft/ 429 m)

POPULATION
4.5 million (July 1996 estimate)

ETHNIC GROUPS
Native Moldovans, Ukrainians, Russians, Gagauz, Bulgarians, Jews, others

MAIN RELIGION
Eastern Orthodox

LANGUAGES
Moldovan, Romanian, Russian, and Gagauz

TYPE OF GOVERNMENT
Republic

HEAD OF STATE
President Petru Lucinschi

HEAD OF GOVERNMENT
Prime Minister Ion Ciubuc

EXPORTS
Foodstuffs, wine, tobacco, textiles and footwear, machinery, chemicals

IMPORTS
Oil, gas, coal, steel, machinery, foodstuffs, automobiles, and other consumer durables

CURRENCY
The Moldovan leu (plural lei)
MDL 9 = US$1 (Aug 1999)

NATIONAL HOLIDAY
Independence Day: August 27

LEADERS IN THE ARTS
Valentin Koryakin, Vitaliy Tiseev (painting)
Mihai Eminescu (literature)
Ion and Doina Aldea-Teodorovici (music)

GLOSSARY

Agrarian Democratic Party (DAP)
One of the main political parties in Moldova, led by former communists.

baklava ("Ba-KLA-va")
A Turkish pastry with crushed pistachios or almonds.

borsch ("BOR-sher")
A Ukrainian national dish that has become Moldovan's favorite.

brinza ("BRIHN-zah")
Sheep milk cheese cured in brine.

ciorba ("CHOR-ba")
A Moldovan sour-tasting soup.

Commonwealth of Independent States (CIS)
An alliance consisting of former Soviet republics after the fall of communism.

Gagauz ("ga-GA-ooze")
A Christian Turkic minority in Moldova.

glasnost ("GLASS-nos")
The policy of a more open, consultative government.

Gross Domestic Product (GDP)
The total monetary value of goods and services produced in a country in one year.

International Monetary Fund (IMF)
An international organization that promotes stability in the world's currencies and maintains a fund pool from which member nations can draw.

mamaliga ("mah-me-LI-ga")
The national dish of Moldova, made of corn.

mititei ("me-tee-TAY")
A traditional dish consisting of grilled meatballs.

North Atlantic Treaty Organization (NATO)
An organization formed for the purpose of collective defense against aggression.

perestroika ("perry-STROT-car")
The policy of reforming the economic and political system.

placinte ("pla-CHIN-te")
A Moldovan type of turnover.

Union of the Soviet Socialist Republics (USSR)
Official name of the former Soviet Union.

United Nations (UN)
An international organization formed to promote international peace, security, and cooperation.

zakazinki ("ZA-GA-zinc-kee")
A botanical santuary.

BIBLIOGRAPHY

Abel, Elie. *The Shattered Bloc*. Houghton, 1990.

Dyer, Donald Leroy. *Studies in Moldovan*. East European Monographs No 454, 1996.

Kelly, Robert C. *Country Review, Moldova*. Commercial Data International, Inc., 1998.

King, Charles. *Post-Soviet Moldova*. Center for Romanian Studies, 1997.

Moldova—A Country Study Guide: Basic Information for Research and Pleasure. Russian Information and Business Center, Incorporated, 1999.

Moldova Then and Now. Minneapolis, Minnesota: Lerner Publications, 1993.

Williams, Nicola and St. Vincent, David. *Romania and Moldova (1st Edition)*. Lonely Planet Publications, 1998.

INDEX

abortion, 66
Academy of Music, 94
Africa, 74
Agrarian Democratic Party (DAP), 24, 35, 39
agriculture, 12, 42–43, 45, 47, 49, 50, 115
animals, 10, 11, 13
architecture, 78
army, 24, 33
Autonomous Soviet Socialist Republic, 26, 28

Balanesti, Mount, 7
Belarus, 93
Bessarabia, 19–21, 54
Bessarabian Metropolitan Church (BMC), 75
birds, 11
births, 62
Black Sea, 8, 19
Bolshevik Revolution, 21
books, 86, 98
bread, 116, 117
Brezhnev, Leonid, 22, 76
Bulgarians, 55, 56
Byzantine Empire, 78, 91, 110

Canada, 93
cancer, 68, 69
Cave Monastery, 81
children, 53, 57, 61, 66, 67, 69, 73, 99, 104, 105
China, 101
Chisinau Oncological Institute, 68
Christmas Day, 109, 110
church, 7, 22, 62, 73, 76–80, 93, 108, 110, 111
cinema, 102
cities:
    Balti, 54
    Capriana, 45, 81
    Causeni, 73
    Chisinau, 21, 45, 48, 54, 67, 71, 73, 75, 81, 89, 92–98, 101, 107, 115, 121
    Saharna, 81
    Soroca, 45
    Tighina, 27, 29, 45, 54
    Tipova, 81
    Tiraspol, 54
Ciubuc, Ion, 35
climate, 9
Codri Hills, 10, 103, 118
Commonwealth of Independent States (CIS), 29, 34, 37, 44, 47

communist, 24, 31, 35, 112
Communist Party, 28, 31, 34, 39, 56
computers, 65
concerts, 101, 102
conservation, 13
constitution, 24
construction, 49
Council of Europe, 36, 71
Council of Ministers, 32
crime, 51, 61, 70
culture, 3, 57
currency, 41, 49
Cyrillic alphabet, 22, 84, 85, 87

Dacians, 19
dance, 91, 98, 112
deer, 11
democracy, 3, 31, 39, 70
demonstrations, 19, 22, 25
drinks, 62, 110, 120
drought, 42, 43

Easter, 108, 109
Eastern Orthodox Church, 20, 62, 73–75, 77–79, 110
Economic Union, 37
education, 61, 64

INDEX

elections, 24, 27, 28, 31, 35
energy, 41, 46
Europe, 3, 20, 37, 45, 53, 74, 94, 95
European Bank of Reconstruction
   and Development, 36
European Union (EU), 36, 37, 70

family, 57, 61, 62, 66, 101, 103, 107,
   108, 109, 115
family planning, 66
fauna, 11
Festival of the Transfiguration, 110–
   111
films, 86
fish, 11
flag, 23, 38
flora, 10
folklore, 92
food, 50, 54, 62, 107, 109, 117
foreign invasions, 19
forests, 7, 10
France, 93
frescoes, 93
fruit, 43, 44, 49, 115, 118
funeral, 62, 63

Gagauz, 25, 28, 31, 34, 55, 83
Gagauzia, 89
games, 101, 105
Germany, 21, 93, 112
glasnost, 23
Gorbachev, Mikhail, 23, 76, 87
graffiti, 71
Greeks, Greece, 19, 74
gross domestic product (GDP), 44,
   49
Guaranteed Minimum of Medical
   Assistance, 66

healthcare, 66
highways, 46, 48
Hitler, Adolf, 21
hospital, 66
housing, 50, 70
human rights, 69
hymns, 80

icons, 78, 79
imports, 11, 49
independence, 3, 19, 20, 23–27, 36, 38,
   39, 41, 55, 69, 96, 104
industry, 44, 49
inflation, 41
infrastructure, 41, 46
International Monetary Fund (IMF), 36
International Planned Parenthood
   Federation (IPPF), 67
international relations, 36
Internet, 61, 65
investment, 45, 40
Israel, 93, 113

Japan, 93
Jews, 55, 73, 113, 121
judiciary, 32

kitchen, 117
Khrushchev, Nikita, 76, 86

languages:
   Bulgarian, 56
   English, 89
   Gagauzian, 28, 87
   Latin, 19, 23, 84
   Moldavian/Moldovan, 22, 23, 25, 28,
      38, 83–85, 87, 89, 98, 99, 101
   Old Slavic, 85
   Russian, 22, 25, 83, 86, 87, 89, 97, 101
   Ukrainian, 38
law, 22, 26, 28, 66, 80, 87
legislative branch, 31, 32
Lenin, 97
life expectancy, 53
literacy rate, 64
Lucinschi, Petru C., 24, 35, 36, 39, 96

market economy, 3, 29, 31, 41
marriage, 62
meals, 101, 116
media, 88
Memorial of Military Glory, 21
men, 58, 104, 105
Middle Ages, 93

Middle East, 20, 74, 77
military, 32, 33
Ministry of Education, 65
Ministry of Health, 68
Ministry of Interior, 33
Ministry of Privatization, 50
minorities, 25, 31, 34, 56, 97
Moldavia, 19–23, 85, 86
Moldovan Metropolitan Church
   (MMC), 73, 75
monasteries, 45, 79, 81, 93
Moscow, 27
mountains, 7
music, 62, 91, 94, 95, 98, 112
Muslims, 77

national costume, 59
national identity, 3
National Philharmonic Society, 95,
   112
natural gas, 46
natural springs, 8
nature reserve, 13
New Year's Day, 107
newspapers, 88, 89, 101

Organization for Security and
   Cooperation in Europe (OSCE),
   37–39
outdoor activities, 103

painting, 93
parliament, 23, 25, 26, 28, 31, 32, 35,
   39, 56, 66, 69
Patriarch of Constantinople, 73, 74
perestroika, 87
policemen, 33, 48
political groups, 23, 34
pollution, 12
Pope of Rome, 74
Popular Front of Moldavia, 23, 34
population, 51, 53–56, 64, 65, 88
pottery, 92
president, 24, 27, 31, 32, 35, 75
prime minister, 23, 32
privatization, 41–43, 50, 65

INDEX

radio, 89, 101
railway, 47, 50
rain, 8, 9
Red Sea, 113
restaurants, 116, 121
rice, 116, 119
rivers:
   Cogalnic, 8
   Danube, 8, 47
   Dniester, 7, 8, 19, 22, 25, 26, 47,
     69, 81
   Ialpug, 8
   Prut, 7, 19, 22, 47
   Raut, 8, 12, 19
river valleys, 8, 12, 19
roads, 46
Roman Catholic Church, 74
Romania, 3, 7, 8, 20, 21–23, 25, 33,
   37, 49, 86, 91
Rome, Romans, 19, 74, 96
rural areas, 54, 61–64, 71, 101, 103
Russia, Russians, 29, 37, 38, 49, 55,
   101, 112
Russian 14th Army, 26, 33, 37
Russian Empire, 20, 21, 78
Russian Federation, 38
Russianization, 19, 22

schools, 64, 65, 85, 87, 104
seasons, 9
Slavs, 83
Snegur, Mircea, 24, 35, 39
social security, 51
Socialist Party, 39
soil erosion, 10
sovereignty, 23, 24, 27, 31, 38
Soviet Union, 19, 23, 41, 43, 53, 54,
   64, 65, 73, 76, 83, 96, 101, 104,
   109, 120
sports, 104, 105
St. Nicholas' Day, 109
Stalin, Josef, 21, 76, 86
standard of living, 41, 54
Stephen the Great, 20, 81, 96
Sturza, Ion, 35, 75
Supreme Court, 32

synagogues, 22

tax, 42
telecommunications, 41, 45, 50
television, 89, 101, 107
theater, 91, 97, 101, 102
tourism, 45
trade, 49
traditional dress, 59, 91
Transnistria, 19, 25–27, 31, 33, 34, 37–39,
   55
transport, 47–50
Treaty of Bucharest, 20
tuberculosis, 67
Turks, 29, 78

Ukraine, 3, 7, 8, 20, 22, 24, 29, 37, 38, 49,
   55, 91, 119
UN Development Program (UNDP), 37
UN Universal Declaration of Human
   Rights, 31
unemployment, 51
Union of Soviet Socialist Republics
   (USSR), 21, 22, 45, 54
United Nations, 29, 31, 37
United States, 45, 49, 53, 65, 93, 94, 98,
   112, 117
university, 65, 96
US Agency for International Development
   (USAID), 50

vegetables, 8, 42, 44, 115, 119
villages, 7, 54, 57, 61, 63, 71, 88, 101

war, 20
wine, 43, 45, 49, 120, 121
women, 37, 58, 59, 66, 68, 69, 83, 104,
   111, 112, 117
Women's Day, 111, 112
woodcarvings, 92, 104
World Bank, 13
World Health Organization (WHO), 67
World Wars, 21, 76, 92, 96

Yeltsin, Boris, 27